Rossiter Worthington Raymond

A Glossary of Mining and Metallurgical Terms

Rossiter Worthington Raymond

A Glossary of Mining and Metallurgical Terms

ISBN/EAN: 9783743345591

Manufactured in Europe, USA, Canada, Australia, Japa

Cover: Foto ©ninafisch / pixelio.de

Manufactured and distributed by brebook publishing software (www.brebook.com)

Rossiter Worthington Raymond

A Glossary of Mining and Metallurgical Terms

A GLOSSARY

OF

MINING AND METALLURGICAL TERMS.

BY

R. W. RAYMOND, Ph.D., NEW YORK.

From Volume IX, Transactions of the American Institute of Mining Engineers.

EASTON, PA.:
PUBLISHED BY THE INSTITUTE,
AT THE OFFICE OF THE SECRETARY, LAFAYETTE COLLEGE.
1881.

A GLOSSARY OF MINING AND METALLURGICAL TERMS.

BY R. W. RAYMOND, PH.D., NEW YORK.

THE absence of a convenient glossary of terms connected with mining and metallurgy has long been felt by the general public. It is to meet this want, not to furnish a technical manual for experts, that the following glossary has been prepared. It originated in an attempt on my part to revise for publication the manuscript of a compilation prepared from the appendix of Yale's work on *Mining Titles* and one or two other sources, to serve as an appendix to a new work on mining law, about to be published by Mr. H. N. Copp, of Washington, D. C. This revision soon assumed, contrary to my original intention, the proportions of a reconstruction; and with the consent of Mr. Copp, and for the purpose of receiving from my fellow-members valuable aid, I presented my still incomplete work as a paper at the Lake Superior meeting of the Institute, inviting from any quarter suggestions of new terms or better definitions to be incorporated in the glossary before its final publication. This invitation was so widely and generously responded to, that I cannot undertake to make in this place individual acknowledgments to those members of the Institute, and professional colleagues outside of it, who have favored me with assistance and advice. The labor bestowed upon this paper since its presentation at the Lake Superior meeting has considerably exceeded that of its first preparation, as may be inferred from its great increase in length, as well as the numerous alterations which it has undergone. It could certainly be still further enlarged and improved; but I think a comparison of it with any of the glossaries of the same class now in print will show, at least, that it is an advance upon what has hitherto been accomplished. I shall be grateful, however, for further criticisms and suggestions; and I purpose at some future time to incorporate in a supplementary paper the results of such additional collections or corrections as I may obtain.

To avoid too great prolixity, I adopted at the outset the following general principles:

1. To include the most important technical words and phrases used by American miners and metallurgists, or occurring in English books and periodicals.

2. To exclude Spanish, French, and German terms, unless they fall under the rule above given. The Spanish terms included are in use among our miners in the far West and Southwest.

3. To exclude almost all purely scientific terms, such as those which denote the operations of chemical analysis, the chemical names and symbols of elements and compounds, the species of rocks and minerals, the principles of general physics and mechanics, etc.

4. To avoid scientific and technical explanations.

5. To omit, in general, self-explanatory terms, and such as are common to all mechanical and manufacturing trades.

The grounds of these rules are evident. It was neither practicable nor necessary to give in this paper what could be, and must be, sought in technical textbooks or general dictionaries and cyclopædias. But the paper as presented, and to a still higher degree as now completed, presents numerous exceptions to the above rules. Many geological terms, for instance, are so common among miners, and many chemical terms are so common among metallurgists as to render their adoption in this catalogue justifiable. The difficulty has been to "draw the line;" and this has been done, as I must confess, somewhat arbitrarily, and rather under the influence of a desire not to overburden the *Transactions* of the Institute than in consistent obedience to any rule.

An apology should be made for the obscurity of a few of the definitions. Many terms taken from English glossaries were found to be most vaguely defined; and in most cases of this kind, I was able to improve the definitions; but there remain some with which I was neither sufficiently acquainted to amend them with certainty, nor sufficiently dissatisfied to strike them out altogether, nor sufficiently satisfied to let them stand without any explanation.

In many instances, the locality in which a term is believed to have originated or to be peculiarly in use, is indicated by abbreviations which will mostly explain themselves. The principal regions named are England, Scotland, Wales, France, Germany, the United States, Spain (including Mexico), Australia, Cornwall, Derbyshire, Staffordshire, Newcastle, Devonshire, Lake Superior, Pennsylvania, and the Pacific slope (including the mining districts of the Rocky Mountains). It must be understood that the naming, in this connection, of any one locality does not exclude the use of the term in other localities; and particularly that in this country the circulation both of miners and metallurgists, and of books and journals from all the world has brought into use a heterogeneous technical vocabulary. This is especially the case in the gold, silver, and lead mining districts of the West, where all the names, phrases, and theories that anybody anywhere at any time has cultivated, together with a crop of indigenous, spontaneous growth, seem to flourish vigorously.

GLOSSARY.

Abstrich, GERM. The black or greenish-brown mass (*black litharge*) appearing upon the bath of work-lead early in the cupelling-process, and gradually, as the process advances, giving way to pure litharge.

Abzug, GERM. The first scum appearing (before the *abstrich*) on the surface of molten lead.

Adit. A nearly horizontal passage from the surface, by which a mine is entered and unwatered. In the United States an adit is usually called a *tunnel*, though the latter, strictly speaking, passes entirely through a hill, and is open at both ends.

Adlings, ENG. Earnings.

Adobe, SP. Clay suitable for *adobes* or sun-dried bricks.

Adventurers, ENG. Shareholders or partners in a mining enterprise; in Cornwall, *cost-book* partners.

After-damp, ENG. The irrespirable gas, consisting of nitrogen and carbonic acid chiefly, remaining after an explosion of *fire-damp*.

Agitator, PAC. See *Settler*.

Aich's metal. See *Gun-metal*.

Air-head, or *Air-heading*, S. STAF. A smaller passage, driven parallel with the *gate-road*, and near its roof, to carry the ventilating current. It is connected with the *gate-road* at intervals by openings called *spouts*.

Air-reduction process. See *Roasting and Reaction process*.

Aitch-piece. See *H-piece*.

Alberti furnace. A continuously working reverberatory furnace for the roasting of quicksilver ores, with condensation of the mercury in iron-tubes and brick chambers.

Alligator. 1. See *Squeezer*. 2. A rock-breaker operating by jaws.

Alloy. A compound of two or more metals fused together.

Alluvium. The earthy deposit made by running streams, especially in times of flood.

Aludel. An earthen condenser for mercury. See *Bustamente furnace*.

Aluminium ores. Cryolite, a fluoride of sodium and aluminium, found in Greenland; *bauxite*, a hydrous compound of alumina, ferric oxide and silica.

Amalgamation. 1. The production of an amalgam or alloy of mercury. 2. The process in which gold and silver are extracted from pulverized ores by producing an amalgam, from which the mercury is afterwards expelled. See *Retorting*.

Amalgamator. 1. A machine for amalgamating ores. 2. The workmen in charge of such a machine.

American forge. See *Catalan forge*.

Anemometer. An instrument for measuring the rapidity of an air-current.

Annealing. 1. The gradual cooling of glass or metal from a high temperature, to render it less brittle. 2. See *Malleable castings*.

Anthracite. See *Coal*.

Anticlinal. The line of a crest, above or under ground, on the two sides of which the strata dip in opposite directions. The converse of *synclinal*.

Antimony ores. Native antimony; *stibnite* (sulphide of antimony); *valentinite* and *senarmontite* (oxides).

Apex. In the U.S. Revenue Statutes, the end or edge of a vein nearest the surface.

Apolvillados, Sp. Ores superior in quality to the *azogues*.

Appolt oven. An oven for the manufacture of coke, differing from the *Belgian* in that it is divided into vertical compartments.

Aprons. See *Copper-plates*.

Arch, Corn. 1. A portion of a lode left standing when the rest is extracted, to support the *hanging wall* or because it is too poor for profitable extraction. 2. The roof of a reverberatory furnace.

Arenaceous. Silicious or sandy (of rocks).

Arends' tap. An arrangement by which the molten lead from the crucible of a shaft-furnace is drawn through an "inverted siphon" into an exterior basin, from which it can be ladled without disturbing the furnace.

Arenillos, Sp. Refuse earth.

Argentiferous. Containing silver.

Argillaceous. Containing clay.

Arm. The inclined member or leg of a set or frame of timber.

Arrastre, Sp. Apparatus for grinding and mixing ores by means of a heavy stone dragged around upon a circular bed. The arrastre is chiefly used for ores containing free gold, and amalgamation is combined with the grinding. Sometimes incorrectly written *arraster*, *arrastra*, or *raster*.

Arroba, Sp. Twenty-five pound avoirdupois.

Arsenic ores. Native arsenic; *mispickel* (*arsenopyrite, arsenical Pyrites*, arseno-sulphide of iron).

Ascension-theory. The theory that the matter filling fissure-veins was introduced in solution from below.

Ash-pit. The receptacle for ashes under a fire-place.

Assay. To test ores and minerals by chemical or blowpipe examination; said to be in *the dry way* when done by means of heat (as in a crucible), and in *the wet or humid way* when by means of solution and precipitation or liquid tests. An assay differs from a complete analysis in being confined to the determination of certain ingredients, the rest not being determined. Both assays and analyses may be either qualitative or quantitative; that is, they may determine the presence merely, or also the amount, of some or all of the constituents of the substance examined. The assay value of gold and silver ores is usually determined in Troy ounces (or, for gold, pennyweights) per ton (2000 pounds avoirdupois) of ore. See *Assay ton*. When reported in money value, the ounce of gold is taken at \$20.6718. A ton of pure gold would be worth \$602,928.51; the value of \$6 per ton would be by weight one-thousandth per cent., and so on. Silver varies greatly in market value; but assayers often report their results according to the old U.S. standard, which made the ounce of pure silver worth \$1.2929. The ton of silver at this rate, would be worth \$37,710.40; the value of \$37 per ton would be by weight one-tenth per cent., and so on. For ordinary gold and silver ores, it is evident that the percentages would be inconveniently small as expressions of value. Assays of lead, copper, iron, etc., are reported in percentages.

Assay-ton. A weight of 29.166⅔ grams. Since one ton of 2000 pounds avoirdupois contains 29.166⅔ troy ounces, it is evident that each milligram of gold or silver obtained from one *assay-ton* of ore represents one ounce troy to the ton of 2000 pounds avoirdupois.

Assessment-work, Pac. The work done annually on a mining claim to maintain possessory title.

Astel. Overhead boarding or arching in a gallery.

Astyllen, Eng. A small dam in an adit or level, to check water.

Atierres, Sp. Refuse ores.

Attle, Corn. Refuse rock.

Auger-nose shell. See *Wimble*.

Auger-stem. The bar to which a *drilling-bit* is attached.
Augêt or *Augêtte.* A priming tube, used in blasting.
Augustin process. The treatment of silver ores by chloridizing, roasting, lixiviation with hot brine, and precipitation with copper.
Auriferous. Containing gold.
Average produce, Corn. The quantity of pure or fine copper in one hundred parts of ore.
Average standard, Corn. The price per ton of pure or fine copper in the ore.
Aviador, Sp. A person who *habilitates* a mine; that is, who furnishes the money for working it by a contract with proprietors.
Azogueria, Sp. 1. The amalgamating works. 2. The processs of amalgamation.
Azogues, Sp. Common or inferior ores.

Back, Corn. 1. With reference to an adit, drift or stope, the part of the vein between it and the next working above, or the surface. 2. See *Face.*
Back-casing, Eng. A temporary shaft-lining of bricks laid dry, and supported at intervals upon *curbs.* When the *stone-head* has been reached, the permanent masonry lining is built upon it inside of the *back-casing.*
Back-end, Newc. The part of a *judd* remaining after the *sump* has been removed.
Backing deals, Newc. Planks driven vertically behind the curbs in a shaft from one curb to another.
Back-shift. The second set of miners working in any spot each day.
Back-skin, Newc. A leather covering worn by men in wet workings.
Bait, Newc. A pitman's provisions.
Bal, Corn. A mine.
Balance-bob. A heavy lever ballasted at one end, and attached at the other to the pump-rod, the weight of which it thus helps to carry. When the shaft is deep, and the pump-rods are consequently very heavy, balance-bobs are put in at intervals of 200 or 300 feet, thus relieving the strain on the rods themselves and on the engine.
Balk, Newc. A *hitch* producing a *nip.*
Balland, Derb. Pulverulent lead ore.
Ballast-shovel. A round-mouthed shovel.

Balling. The aggregation of iron in the *puddling* or the *bloomary* process into *balls* or *loups*.

Ball-stamp, Lake Sup. A stamp for crushing rock, operated directly by steam-power, the stem of the stamp being at the same time the piston-rod of a steam cylinder.

Band, Newc. Stone interstratified with coal.

Bank 1. (Derb. or *Benk*). The face of the coal at which miners are working. 2. An ore-deposit or coal-bed worked by surface excavations or drifts above water-level. 3. Eng. The ground at the top of a shaft. Ores are brought "to bank," *i. e.,* "to grass." See *Grass*.

Banksman, Newc. See *Lander*.

Bar. 1. A drilling or tamping-rod. 2. A vein or dike crossing a lode. 3. A sand or rock ridge crossing the bed of a stream.

Bar-diggings, Pac. Gold-washing claims located on the bars (shallows) of a stream, and worked when the water is low, or otherwise with the aid of coffer-dams.

Barilla, Sp. Native copper disseminated in grains in copper ores.

Barmaster, Derb. A mining official who collects the dues or royalties, presides over the *barmote*, etc. (From *Germ. Bergmeister*.)

Barmote, Derb. A mining court.

Barney. A small car attached to a rope and used to push cars up a slope or inclined plane.

Barranca, Sp. A ravine.

Barrel. 1. The water-cylinder of a pump. 2. A piece of small pipe inserted in the end of a cartridge to carry the *squib* to the powder. 3. A vessel used in amalgamation.

Barrel-amalgamation. The amalgamation of silver ores by revolution in wooden barrels with quicksilver, metallic iron, and water.

Barrel-work, Lake Sup. Native copper occurring in pieces of a size to be sorted out by hand in sufficient purity for smelting without mechanical concentration.

Barrier-pillars. Pillars of coal, larger than ordinary, left at intervals to prevent too extensive crushing when the ground comes to be *robbed*.

Barrow, Corn. 1. A heap of *attle* or rubbish; a *dump*. 2. A vehicle in which ore, coal, etc., are wheeled.

Barrowmen, Newc. See *Putters*.

Barrow-way, Newc. A *level* through which coal or ore is wheeled.

Base bullion. See *Bullion.*

Base metals. The metals not classed as *noble* or precious. See *Noble metals.*

Basic. In furnace practice, a slag in which the earthy bases are in excess of the amount required to form a neutral slag with the silica present.

Basic lining. A lining for furnaces, converters, etc., formed of non-silicious material, usually limestone, dolomite, lime, magnesia, or iron oxide.

Basic-lining process. An improvement of the *Bessemer process*, in which, by the use of a basic lining in the *converter* and by the addition of basic materials during the *blow*, it is possible to eliminate phosphorus from the pig iron, and keep it out of the steel.

Basin. 1. A natural depression of strata containing a coal bed or other stratified deposit. 2. The deposit itself.

Bass or *batt.* See *Bind.*

Basset, DERB. An outcrop; the edge of a stratum.

Batch, CORN. The quantity of ore sent to the surface by a *pare* of men.

Batea, SP. A large wooden bowl in which gold-bearing earth or crushed ore is washed in the same way as in a *pan.*

Bath. A mass of molten material in a furnace, or of solution in a tank.

Batt. See *Bind.*

Battery. 1. A set of *stamps* in a stamp-mill, comprising the number which fall in one *mortar*, usually five. 2. A bulkhead of timber. 3. The plank closing the bottom of a *coal-chute.*

Battery-amalgamation. Amalgamation by means of mercury placed in the mortar.

Battery-assay. See *Pulp-assay.*

Bauxite. See *Aluminium-ores.*

Beans, NEWC. Small coals.

Bean-shot. Copper granulated by pouring into hot water.

Bear. 1. See *Salamander.* 2. See *Loup.*

Bearing. See *Strike.*

Bed. A seam or deposit of mineral, later in origin than the rock below, and older than the rock above; that is to say, a regular member of the series of formations, and not an intrusion.

Bedded vein. Properly *bed-vein* (*Lagergang* of the Germans); a lode occupying the position of a bed, that is, parallel with the stratification of the inclosing rocks.

Bede. A miner's pickaxe.
Bed-rock, Pac. The solid rock underlying alluvial and other surface formations.
Bed-way. An appearance of stratification, or parallel marking, in granite.
Beehive oven. An oven for the manufacture of coke, shaped like the old-fashioned beehive.
Belgian oven. A rectangular oven with end-doors and side-flues for the manufacture of coke.
Belgian zinc-furnace. A furnace in which zinc is reduced and distilled from calcined ores in tubular retorts.
Bell and hopper. See *Cup and cone.*
Belly-helve, Eng. A forge-hammer, lifted by a cam which acts about midway between the fulcrum and the head.
Bell-metal. A hard bronze, containing sometimes small proportions of iron, zinc, or lead, but ordinarily consisting of 78 parts copper to 22 tin.
Bell's dephosphorizing process. The removal of phosphorus from molten pig iron in a puddling furnace, lined with iron oxide and fitted with a mechanical rabble to agitate the bath. Red-hot iron ore is added. See *Krupp's washing process.*
Bench. 1. One of two or more divisions of a coal seam, separated by slate, etc., or simply separated by the process of cutting the coal, one bench or layer being cut before the adjacent one. 2. To cut the coal in *benches.*
Benching-up, Newc. Working on the top of coal.
Bend or *Bind,* Derb. Indurated clay.
Beneficiar, Sp. To benefit. To work or improve a mine; to reduce its ores; to derive profit or advantage from working it. *Beneficiation,* sometimes used in English, usually means the reduction of ores.
Bessemer iron. Pig iron suitable for the Bessemer process.
Bessemer process. The process of decarburizing a bath of molten cast iron by blowing air through it, in a vessel called a *converter.*
Biche. A tool ending below in a conical cavity, for recovering broken rods from a bore-hole.
Billet. 1. Iron or steel, drawn from a pile, bloom, or ingot into a small bar for further manufacture. 2. A small bloom.
Bind, Derb. See *Bend.*
Bing, North Eng. Eight hundred weight of ore.
Bing-ore, Derb. Ore in lumps.

Bing-hole, DERB. A hole or *shoot* through which ore is thrown.
Bing-tale, NORTH ENG. See *Tribute*.
Bismuth-ores. Native bismuth; *bismuth ochre* (oxide); *bismuthine* (sulphide); also, bismuthiferous cobalt, silver and copper ores.
Bit. The cutting end of a boring implement.
Bituminous coal. See *Coal*.
Black-band. An earthy carbonate of iron, accompanying coal-beds. Extensively worked as an iron ore in Great Britain, and somewhat in Ohio.
Black-copper. Impure copper from smelting, before refining.
Black-damp, ENG. Carbonic acid gas.
Black-ends, ENG. Refuse coke from coking-ovens.
Black-flux. A mixture of charcoal and potassium carbonate.
Black-jack, CORN. Zinc-blende; sometimes hornblende.
Black-lead. Graphite.
Black litharge. See *Abstrich*.
Black-plate. Sheet iron before tinning.
Black-tin, CORN. Tin ore prepared for smelting.
Blair process. An improved form of the *Chenot process*.
Blanch. Lead ore, mixed with other minerals.
Blanched copper. An alloy of copper and arsenic.
Blanket-sluices. Sluices in which coarse blankets are laid, to catch the fine but heavy particles of gold, amalgam, etc., in the slime passing over them. The blankets are removed and washed from time to time, to obtain the precious metal.
Blast. 1. The operation of *blasting*, or rending rock or earth by means of explosions. 2. The air forced into a furnace to accelerate combustion. 3. The period during which a blast furnace is *in blast*, that is, in operation.
Blast furnace. A furnace, usually a shaft-furnace, into which air is forced under pressure.
Blasting-stick. A simple form of fuse.
Bleaching-clay, CORN. Kaolin, used with size, to whiten and give weight and substance to cotton goods.
Bleiberg furnace. See *Carinthian furnace*.
Blende. See *Zinc-ores*.
Blick, GERM. The *brightening* or iridescence appearing on silver or gold at the end of the cupelling or refining process.
Blind level. 1. A level not yet connected with other workings. 2. A level for drainage, having a shaft at either end, and acting as an inverted siphon.

Blind-shaft. See *Winze.*
Blister-steel. See *Steel.*
Bloat. A hammer swelled at the eye.
Block-coal, U. S. See *Coal.*
Block-furnace. See *Bloomary.*
Block-tin. Cast tin.
Bloom. 1. A large steel bar, drawn from an ingot for further manufacture. 2. A rough bar of iron, drawn from a Catalan or bloomary ball, for further manufacture. See *Billet.*
Bloomary. A forge for making wrought-iron, usually direct from the ore. The sides are iron plates, the *hair-plate* at the back, the *cinder-plate* at the front, the *tuyere-plate* (through which the tuyere passes) at one side (its upper part being called in some bloomaries the *merrit-plate*) the *fore-spar plate* opposite the *tuyere-plate* (its upper part being the *skew-plate*) and the *bottom-plate* at the bottom.
Blossom. The oxidized or decomposed outcrop of a vein or coalbed, more frequently the latter. Also called *smut* and *tailing.* See *Gossan.*
Blow. A single *heat* or operation of the Bessemer *converter.*
Blower, NEWC. 1. A strong discharge of gas from a fissure. 2. A *fan* or other apparatus for forcing air into a furnace or mine.
Blow-george. A hand-fan.
Blow-in. To put a blast furnace in operation.
Blow-out. 1. To put a blast furnace out of blast, by ceasing to charge fresh materials, and continuing the blast until the contents of the furnace have been smelted. 2. A large outcrop, beneath which the vein is smaller, is called a *blow-out.* 3. A *shot* or blast is said to *blow out* when it goes off like a gun and does not shatter the rock.
Blowpipe. A tube through which air is forced into a flame, to direct it and increase its intensity. In the compound blowpipe, two jets of gas (one of which may be air) are united at the point of combustion.
Blue-billy, ENG. The residuum of cupreous pyrites after roasting with salt.
Blue-john, DERB. Fluorspar.
Blue lead. (Pronounced like the verb *to lead.*) The bluish auriferous gravel and cement deposit found in the ancient river-channels of California.
Blue metal. See *Metal.*

Blue peach, CORN. A slate-blue, very fine-grained schorl-rock.

Bluestone. Copper-vitriol; copper-sulphate.

Boards. The first set of excavations in *post-and-stall* work.

Boat level, WALES. A navigable *adit*.

Bob, CORN. A triangular frame, by means of which the horizontal motion imparted from an engine is transformed into a vertical motion of the pump-rods in a shaft.

Bob-station. See *Station*.

Bog-iron ore. A loose, earthy *brown hematite*, of recent origin, formed in swampy ground.

Boiling. See *Puddling*.

Bonanza, SP. Literally, fair weather. In miners' phrase, good luck, or a body of rich ore. A mine is *in bonanza* when it is profitably producing ore.

Bone. The slaty matter intercalated in coal-seams.

Bonnet. A covering over a cage to shield it from objects falling down the shaft.

Bonney, CORN. An isolated body of ore.

Booming. The accumulation and sudden discharge of a quantity of water (in placer mining, where water is scarce). See, also, *Hushing*.

Boot. A leather or tin joint connecting the *blast-main* with the *tuyère* or *nozzle* in a *bloomary*.

Bord, NEWC. A passage or *breast*, driven up the slope of the coal from the gangway, and hence across the *grain* of the coal.

Bord. See *Boards, Breast*, and *Post-and-stall*.

Board-and-pillar. See *Post-and-stall*.

Borer. See *Drill*.

Borrasca, SP. The converse of *bonanza*. Barren rock.

Bort. Opaque black diamond.

Bosh. 1. A trough in which bloomary tools (or, in copper-smelting, hot ingots) are cooled. 2. (Or, *Boshes*.) The portion of a shaft furnace in which it widens from above the hearth up to its maximum diameter.

Bottom-lift. The deepest lift of a mining-pump, or the lowest pump.

Bottomer, ENG. The man stationed at the bottom of a shaft in charge of the proper loading of cages, signals for hoisting, etc.

Bottoms, CORN. 1. The deepest workings. 2. In copper-smelting, the impure metallic copper, or cupriferous alloy, which separates from the *matt*, and is found below it, when there is not enough sulphur present to retain in combination all the copper.

Boulder or **Bowlder**. A fragment of rock brought by natural means from a distance (though this notion of transportation from a distance is not always, in later usage, involved) and usually large and rounded in shape. *Cobble stones* taken from river-beds are, in some American localities, called boulders.

Bounds, CORN. A tract of tin-ore ground.

Bout, DERB. A measure of lead-ore; twenty-four *dishes*.

Bowke, S. STAFF. A small wooden box in which iron-ore is hauled underground.

Bowse or **Bouze**, DERB. Lead-ore as cut from the lode.

Box-bill. A tool used in deep boring for slipping over and recovering broken rods.

Box-groove. A closed groove between two *rolls*, formed by a collar on one roll, fitting between collars on another roll.

Box-timbering. See *Plank timbering*.

Brace, CORN. The mouth of a shaft.

Brace-head. A cross-attachment at the top of the column of rods in deep boring, by means of which the rods and bit are turned after each drop.

Brace-key. See *Brace-head*.

Braize, U. S. Charcoal-dust. See *Breeze*.

Brake-sieve. A *jigger*, operated by a hand-lever.

Brakesman. The man in charge of a winding-engine.

Brances. See *Brasses*.

Branch. CORN. A small vein departing from the main lode, and in some cases returning.

Basque. A lining for crucibles or furnaces; generally a compound of clay, etc., with charcoal-dust.

Brass. An alloy of copper and zinc.

Brasses, ENG. and WALES. Pyrites (sulphide of iron) in coal.

Brat, ENG. and WALES. A thin bed of coal mixed with pyrites or carbonate of lime.

Brattice, ENG., SCOT., and WALES. A plank lining, or a longitudinal partition of wood, brick, or even cloth, in a shaft, level, or gangway, generally to aid ventilation.

Brazil. Iron pyrites.

Breaker. See *Coal-breaker* and *Rock-breaker*.

Breast. 1. The *face* of a working. 2. In coal mines, the chamber driven upwards from the *gangway*, on the seam, between pillars of coal left standing, for the extraction of coal. 3. That side of the *hearth* of a *shaft-furnace* which contains the *metal-notch*.

Breast-boards. Planking placed between the last set of timbers and the *face* of a *gangway* or *heading* which is in quicksand or loose ground.

Breccia. A conglomerate in which the fragments are angular.

Breeding-fire. See *Gob-fire*.

Breeze, ENG. Small coke. Probably connected, perhaps interchangeable, with *Braize*, and both with the FR. *Braise*.

Brettis, DERB. A crib of timber filled up with slack or waste.

Brettis-way. A road in a coal-mine, supported by *brettises* built on each side after the coal has been worked out.

Bridge. See *Reverberatory furnace*.

Bridle-chains. Safety-chains to support a *cage* if the link between the cage and rope should break.

Brightening. See *Blick*.

Broaching-bit. A tool used to restore the dimensions of a borehole which has been contracted by the swelling of the marl or clay walls.

Brob. A peculiar spike, driven alongside the end of an abutting timber to prevent its slipping.

Broil or *Broyl*, CORN. See *Bryle*.

Broken coal, PENN. See *Coal*.

Bronze. An alloy of copper and tin.

Brood, CORN. The heavier kinds of waste in tin and copper ores.

Brown coal. See *Coal*.

Browse. Ore imperfectly smelted, mixed with cinder and clay.

Brückner cylinder, PAC. A form of revolving roasting furnace.

Bryle, CORN. The traces of a vein, in loose matter, on or near the surface.

Bucker, DERB. A flat piece of iron with a wooden handle, used for breaking ore.

Bucket. The piston of a lifting-pump.

Bucking, DERB. See *Cobbing*. The *bucking-hammer* or *bucking-iron* is a broad-headed hammer used for this purpose; and the ore is broken on a flat piece of iron (*bucking-plate*).

Buckshot-cinder. Cinder from the iron blast-furnace, containing grains of iron.

Buckwheat-coal, PENN. See *Coal*.

Buddle, CORN. An inclined vat or stationary or revolving platform upon which ore is concentrated by means of running water.

Strictly the *buddle* is a shallow vat, not a platform or *table;* at least not in some localities. But general usage, particularly on the Pacific slope, makes no distinction.

Buggy. A small mine-wagon holding ½ ton to 1 ton of coal.

Buhrstone. A quartz rock containing cellules.

Buitron, Sp. A furnace of peculiar construction, in which silver ore is reduced.

Bulkhead. 1. A tight partition or stopping in a mine for protection against water, fire, or gas. 2. The end of a flume, whence water is carried in iron pipes to hydraulic workings.

Bull. See *Clay-iron.*

Bulldog. 1. A refractory material used as furnace-lining, got by calcining *mill-cinder*, and containing silica and ferric oxide. 2. Penn. See *Buckshot-cinder.*

Bullfrog. See *Barney.*

Bullion. Uncoined gold and silver. *Base bullion* (Pac.), is pig lead containing silver and some gold, which are separated by refining.

Bull-pump, Corn. A direct single-acting pump, the steam cylinder of which is placed over the top of a shaft or slope, and the piston-rod attached to the pump-rods. The steam lifts piston and pump-rods, and the weight of these makes the down-stroke.

Bull-wheel. In rope-boring, a wheel on which is wound the rope for hoisting the bit, etc.

Bully. A pattern of miners' hammer, varying from "*broad-bully*" to "*narrow-bully.*"

Bunch of ore, Corn. An ore-body, usually a small one.

Bunding. A staging of boards on *stulls* or *stemples*, to carry *deads.* See *stull-covering.*

Buntons, Eng. Battens or scantlings placed horizontally across a shaft, to which are nailed the boards forming the *cleading* or *sheathing* of a *brattice.*

Burden, Corn. 1. The tops or heads of stream-work, which lie over the stream of tin. 2. The proportion of ore and flux to fuel in the charge of a blast-furnace.

Burning. See *Calcining.*

Burnt iron. 1. Iron which by long exposure to heat has suffered a change of structure and become brittle. It can be restored by careful forging at welding-heat. 2. In the *Bessemer* and open-hearth processes, iron which has been exposed to oxidation until all its carbon is gone, and oxide of iron has been formed in the mass.

Burr. Solid rock.

Burrow, CORN. A heap of refuse.

Buscones, SP. Searchers; explorers.

Bushel. The Imperial bushel, of 2218 cubic inches, and the Winchester bushel, of 2150 cubic inches, are divided into 4 pecks. The bushel used in measuring charcoal and coal contains 5 pecks, or 2680 cubic inches, being 20 pounds or less of charcoal, and, in various localities, 80, 76, or 72 pounds of coal.

Bustamente furnace. A cylindrical shaft-furnace for roasting quicksilver ores; divided by perforated arches into two compartments, of which the upper receives the ore and the lower the fuel. The mercury-vapors are condensed in *aludeln*.

Butt, ENG. Of coal; a surface exposed at right angles to the *face*. See *End*.

Button. The globule of metal remaining on an *assay-cupel* or in a crucible, at the end of the fusion.

Butty, DERB. and STAFF. A miner by contract at so much per ton of coal or ore.

Cabbling. Breaking up pieces of flat iron to be *piled* or *fagoted*, heated and rolled.

Cable-tools. The apparatus used in drilling deep holes, such as artesian wells, with a rope, instead of rods, to connect the drill with the machine on the surface.

Cache, FR. The place where provisions, ammunition, etc., are *cached* or hidden by trappers or prospectors in unsettled regions.

Cage. 1. A frame with one or more platforms for cars, used in hoisting in a vertical shaft. It is steadied by guides on the sides of the shaft. 2. A structure of elastic iron rods slipped into the bore-hole in *rod-boring* to prevent vibration of the rods. 3. The barrel or drum in a *whim* on which the rope is wound.

Cake-copper. See *Tough cake*.

Caking coal. See *Coal*.

Cala, SP. A small pit or experimental hole.

Cal, CORN. Wolfram.

Calcine. To expose to heat, with or without oxidation; to *roast*. Applied to ores for the removal of water and sulphur, and the disintegration of the mass; to limestone for the expulsion of its carbonic acid; etc.

Calciner. A furnace or kiln for roasting.

Calicata, SP. A digging or trial pit.

Campaign. The period during which a furnace is continuously in operation.

Cañada, Sp. A ravine, or small cañon.

Canch. A part of a bed of stone worked by quarrying.

Cand or *Cann,* Corn. Fluorspar.

Cank, Derb. See *Whinstone.*

Cañon, Sp. A valley, usually precipitous; a gorge.

Cannel coal. See *Coal.*

Cap or *Cap-rock.* Barren vein matter, or a *pinch* in a vein, supposed to overlie ore.

Capel. A composite stone of quartz, schorl, and hornblende.

Capella, Sp. Cupelling furnace.

Captain, Corn. and Wales. The official in immediate charge of the work in a mine.

Carat. 1. A unit employed in weighing diamonds, and equal to $3\frac{1}{6}$ troy grains. A *carat-grain* is one-fourth of a carat. 2. A term employed to distinguish the fineness of a gold alloy, and meaning one-twenty-fourth. Fine gold is 24-*carat* gold. Goldsmiths' standard is 22 *carats* fine, *i. e.*, contains 22 parts gold, 1 copper, and 1 silver.

Carbona, Corn. An irregular deposit or impregnation of tin ore, found in connection with a tin lode.

Carbonaceous. Containing carbon not oxidized.

Carbonates. The common term in the West for ores containing a considerable proportion of carbonate of lead. They are sometimes earthy or ochreous (soft carbonates), sometimes granular and comparatively free from iron (sand carbonates), and sometimes compact (hard carbonates.) Often they are rich in silver.

Carbonization. The process of converting to carbon, by removing other ingredients, a substance containing carbon, as in the charring of wood or the natural formation of anthracite.

Carburization. The process of imparting carbon, as in making cement steel.

Carga, Sp. A mule-load of 300 pounds avoirdupois.

Carinthian furnace. A small reverberatory with inclined hearth, in which lead ore is treated by *roasting and reaction,* wood being the usual fuel.

Car-wheel iron. See *Chill.*

Case. A small fissure, admitting water into the workings.

Case-harden. To convert iron superficially into steel by partial cementation.

Casing, CORN. 1. A partition or *brattice*, made of *casing-plank*, in a shaft. 2. PAC. *Casings* are zones of material altered by vein-action, and lying between the unaltered country rock and the vein.

Cast-after-cast, CORN. The throwing up of ore from one platform to another successively. See *Shambles*.

Cast-house. The building in which pigs or ingots are cast.

Casting. Pouring or drawing fused metal from a blast furnace, cupola, crucible, converter, or ladle into moulds.

Cast-iron. See *Iron*.

Cast-steel. See *Steel*.

Cata, SP. A mine denounced, but unworked.

Catalan forge. A forge with a tuyere for reducing iron ore, with charcoal, to a loup of wrought iron; a *bloomary*. See *Champlain forge*.

Cat-head. 1. A small capstan. 2. A *broad-bully* hammer. See *Bully*.

Cauf, NEWC. See *Corf*.

Caunter-lode, CORN. A vein coursing at a considerable angle to neighboring veins.

Caving. The falling in of the sides or top of excavations.

Cawk. Sulphate of baryta (heavy spar).

Cazo, SP. A caldron in which amalgamation is effected by the *cazo* process, used in Mexico and South America.

Cement, AUSTR. and PAC. Gravel firmly held in a silicious matrix, or the matrix itself.

Cementation. The process of producing a chemical change in a solid substance by packing it in a powder and heating it. See *Cement-steel* and *Malleable castings*.

Cement-copper. Copper precipitated from solution.

Cement-gold. Gold precipitated in fine particles from solution.

Cement-silver. Silver precipitated from solution, usually by copper.

Cement-steel. See *Steel*.

Cendrada, SP. Ashes or smeltings found at the bottom of a furnace, and valuable for use in other smeltings.

Cerro, SP. A hill or mountain.

Chacing. Following a vein by its range or direction.

Chafery. A forge fire for *reheating*. (From the FR. *Chaufferie*.)

Chaldron. Thirty-six bushels. In Newcastle fifty-three hundredweight avoirdupois. *Chaldron-wagons*, containing this quantity, convey the coal from the pit to the place of shipment.

Chalybeate. Impregnated with iron (applied to mineral waters).
Chamber. See *Breast.*
Champion lode. The main vein as distinguished from branches.
Champlain forge or *American forge.* A forge for the direct production of wrought iron, generally used in the United States instead of the Catalan forge, from which it differs in using only finely-crushed ore and in working continuously.
Changing-house, CORN. A room where miners change and dry their underground clothing. See *Dry.*
Charbon roux, FR. Brown charcoal, produced by an incomplete carbonization of wood.
Charge. 1. The materials introduced at one time or one round into a furnace. 2. The amount of explosive used for one blast.
Charger, CORN. An auger-like implement for charging horizontal bore-holes for blasting.
Charring. The expulsion by heat of the volatile constituents of wood, etc., leaving more or less pure vegetable carbon.
Chartermaster, S. STAFF. See *Butty.*
Chats, NORTHUMB. Small pieces of stone with ore.
Cheeks. 1. The sides or walls of a vein. 2. Extensions of the sides of the *eye* of a hammer or *pick.*
Chenot process. The process of making *iron-sponge* from ore mixed with coal-dust, and heated in vertical cylindrical retorts.
Chert. Hornstone; a silicious stone often found in limestone.
Cherry coal, ENG. See *Coal.*
Chestnut coal, PENN. See *Coal.*
Chilian Mill. An improved *arrastre,* in which a heavy stone wheel is rolled around the bed.
Chill. An iron mould or portion of a mould, serving to cool rapidly, and so to harden, the surface of molten iron which comes in contact with it. Iron which can be thus hardened to a considerable depth is *chilling iron,* and is specially used for cast-iron railway car-wheels requiring hardness at the rim without loss of strength in the wheel.
Chimming, CORN. See *Tossing.*
Chimney. An ore-shoot. See *Chute.*
China clay. Kaolin.
Chisel. See *Bit.*
Chock. See *Nog.*
Choke-damp, ENG. Carbonic acid gas.

Chlorides, PAC. A common term for ores containing chloride of silver.

Chloridize. To convert into chloride. Applied to the roasting of silver ores with salt, preparatory to amalgamation.

Chlorination process. The process first introduced by Plattner, in which auriferous ores are first roasted to oxidize the base metals, then saturated with chlorine gas, and finally treated with water, which removes the soluble terchloride of gold, to be subsequently precipitated and melted into bars.

Chrome ore. Chromic iron (*chromite*, oxide of chromium and oxide of iron).

Chute. (Sometimes written *shoot.*) 1. A channel or shaft underground, or an inclined trough above ground, through which ore falls or is "shot" by gravity from a higher to a lower level. 2. A body of ore, usually of elongated form, extending downward within a vein (*ore-shoot*). The two forms of orthography of this word are of French and English origin respectively. Under *chute*, the original idea is that of falling; under *shoot*, that of shooting or branching. Both are appropriate to the technical significations of the word. An *ore-shoot*, for instance, may be considered as a branch of the general mass of the ore in a deposit, or as a pitch or fall of ore (GERM. *Erzfall*). In England the orthography *shoot* is, I believe, exclusively employed, and this is perhaps the best, the other being unnecessarily foreign.

Cinder, ENG. Slag, particularly from iron blast furnaces.

Cinder-pig, ENG. See *Pig iron*.

Cinder-plate. See *Bloomary*.

Cinder-tap, Cinder-notch. The hole through which cinder is tapped from a furnace. See *Lürmann front*.

Cinnabar. Sulphuret of mercury.

Cistern, CORN. See *Tank*.

Clack, CORN. A pump-valve.

Clack-door, CORN. An opening into the valve-chamber of a pump.

Claggy, NEWC. Adhesive. When the coal is tightly joined to the roof, the mine is said to have a *claggy top*.

Claim, PAC. The portion of mining ground held under the Federal and local laws by one claimant or association, by virtue of one location and record.

Clanny lamp. The safety-lamp invented by Dr. Clanny.

Clay-iron. A tool for crowding clay into leaky bore-holes.

Cleading, ENG. See *Buntons.*

Clean-up. The operation of collecting all the valuable product of a given period or operation in a stamp mill, or in a hydraulic or placer mine.

Cleat. 1. A joint in coal or rock. 2. A strip of wood.

Cleavage. The property in a mineral, of splitting more easily and perfectly in some directions than in others. The planes of cleavage bear a relation to the crystal form of the mineral. The *cleavage* of rock-masses is more properly a jointing, unless it follows the planes of bedding.

Clinker. The product of the fusion of the earthy impurities (ash) of coal during its combustion.

Clinometer. A simple apparatus for measuring by means of a pendulum or spirit-level and circular scale, vertical angles, particularly *dips.*

Clod. Soft shale or slate, in coal mines, usually applied to a layer forming a bad roof.

Closed top. See *Cup-and-cone.*

Closed front. An arrangement of the blast-furnace without a *fore-hearth.*

Clotting. The sintering or semi-fusion of ores during roasting.

Coal (ENG. *Coals*). This term is now applied to *stonecoal* or *pit-coal,* that is, mineral coal, obtained by mining, as distinguished from charcoal. No scientific account of the nature and origin of coal will be given here. The three principal classes recognized by common usage are *anthracite* (hard, black, composed, when pure, almost exclusively of carbon), *bituminous* or *coking coal* (brown or black, containing hydrocarbons), and *lignite* or *brown coal* (brown or black, generally showing a woody or a laminar structure, containing much water, and more recent, geologically speaking, than the other varieties). *Semi-anthracites* and *semi-bituminous coals* are gradations between *anthracite* and *bituminous,* based on the increasing percentage of volatile matters. *Hydrogenous* or *gas coals* are bituminous coals yielding the highest percentage of volatile matters. The English classification of *bituminous coals* distinguishes *coking coal* proper (splintering when heated, but subsequently fusing into a semi-pasty mass), *cherry* or *soft coal* (igniting readily and burning rapidly without splintering or fusion), *splint, rough* or *hard coal* (igniting with more difficulty but burning with a clear, hot fire), and *cannel coal* (the *parrot coal* of Scotland, compact, homogeneous, conchoidal in fracture, burning with clear, bright flame). The English call *an-*

thracite also *stonecoal* or *culm*, and speak of a *semi-anthracite* as *steam-coal*. Any coal advantageously used for generating steam is called a *steam-coal* in the United States. The solid carbon remaining after the expulsion of volatile matters from *bituminous coal* or *lignite* is called *coke*. Commercial *coke*, however, must have a certain coherence and strength; and the coals which furnish it in this condition are called *coking coals*. A peculiar bituminous coal of Indiana and Ohio, which breaks in blocks, and is used raw without coking, to some extent, as a blast-furnace fuel, is called *block-coal*. *Anthracite* is divided in the United States according to the color of the ash after burning, into *white-ash*, *red-ash*, and *pink-ash coal*. It is also classified for the market according to the size of the pieces (see *Coal-breaker*), as follows: *Lump* includes the largest lumps as they come from the mine. The other sizes pass over and through sieve-meshes of the size named, the figures signifying inches, and thus indicating roughly the average limit of diameter for the pieces in each size, viz.:

Steamboat,	through 7	over 4;
No. 1, *Broken* or *grate*,	through 4	over $2\frac{3}{4}$ to $2\frac{1}{2}$;
No. 2, *Egg*,	through $2\frac{3}{4}$ to $2\frac{1}{2}$	over $2\frac{1}{4}$ to 2;
No. 3, *Large stove*,	through $2\frac{1}{4}$ to 2	over $1\frac{7}{8}$ to $1\frac{1}{2}$;
No. 4, *Small stove*,	through $1\frac{7}{8}$ to $1\frac{1}{2}$	over $1\frac{1}{8}$ to 1;
No. 5, *Chestnut*,	through $1\frac{1}{8}$ to 1	over $\frac{5}{8}$ to $\frac{1}{2}$;
No. 6, *Pea*,	through $\frac{5}{8}$ to $\frac{1}{2}$	over $\frac{3}{8}$ to $\frac{1}{4}$.

No. 7, *Buckwheat*, is rarely made, except when the coal is washed on the screens, and the *chestnut* and *pea* have the larger dimensions above given. It is the smallest size, and usually included in the dirt or *culm*.

Coal-breaker. A building containing the machinery for breaking coal with toothed rolls, sizing it with sieves, and cleaning it for market.

Coal-pipes, NEWC. Very thin irregular layers of coal.

Cobalt-ores. *Cobalt-speiss* (*smaltine, chloanthite* when niccoliferous, *safflorite* when ferriferous, an arsenide of cobalt with or without nickel or iron); *cobalt glance* and *cobalt pyrites* (*smaltite* and *linnæite*, sulphides of cobalt); *cobalt bloom* (*erythrite*, arseniate of cobalt).

Cobbing, CORN. Breaking ore to sort out its better portions. See *Spall*.

Cobble, PENN. An imperfectly puddled ball which goes to pieces in the *squeezer*.

Cobre ores. Copper ores from Cuba.

Cockle, Corn. See *Schorl*.

Cod, Newc. The bearing of an axle.

Coffer or *Cofer*, Derb. 1. To secure a shaft from leaking by ramming in clay behind the masonry or timbering. 2. (or *Cover*) Corn. See *Mortar* (2). 3. A rectangular plank frame, used in timbering *levels*.

Coffin, Corn. 1. An old open working. 2. The mode of open working by casting up ore and waste from one platform to another, and so to the surface.

Cog. To roll or *bloom* ingots.

Cogs. See *Nogs*; only *cogs* are not squared, but simply notched where they cross each other. The interior of a structure of this kind and the spaces between the timber are usually filled with *gob*. They are called also *cobs*, *corncobs*, etc.

Coil-drag. A tool to pick up pebbles, bits of iron, etc., from the bottom of a drill-hole.

Coke. The product remaining after the expulsion by heat of the volatile constituents of coal.

Coking coal. See *Coal*.

Cold-bed. A platform in a rolling-mill on which cold bars are stored.

Cold blast. Air forced into a furnace without being previously heated.

Cold-short. Brittle when cold. Applied chiefly to iron and steel.

Collar. 1. See *Cap*. 2. The *collar* of a shaft is the horizontal timbering around the mouth.

Colliery. A coal mine.

Collom washer, Lake Sup. A variety of *jig*.

Color, Sp. 1. Color. The shade or tint of the earth or rock which indicates ore. 2. A particle of metallic gold found in the prospector's pan after a sample of earth or crushed rock has been "panned out." Prospectors say, e. g., "The dirt gave me so many colors to the panful."

Colorados, Sp. Ores impregnated with oxide of iron, and in a state of decomposition. See *Gossan*.

Col-rake. A shovel used to stir lead-ores during washing.

Comb. The place, in a fissure which has been filled by successive depositions of mineral on the walls, where the two sets of layers thus deposited approach most nearly or meet, closing the fissure and exhibiting either a drusy central cavity, or an interlocking of crystals.

Combined carbon. That portion of the carbon in iron or steel which is not visible as graphite, and is supposed to be alloyed or chemically combined with the iron.

Compass. An instrument like the ordinary nautical or surveyor's compass, though sometimes otherwise marked, and having a *clinometer* attached. Also, a *dip-compass*, for tracing magnetic iron ore, having a needle hung to move in a vertical plane.

Concentration. The removal by mechanical means of the lighter and less valuable portions of ore.

Concentrator. An apparatus in which, by the aid of water or air and specific gravity, mechanical concentration of ores is performed.

Condenser. A vessel or chamber in which volatile products of roasting or smelting (*e. g.*, mercury or zinc vapors) are reduced to solid form by cooling, or in which the fumes of furnaces, containing mechanically suspended as well as volatile metallic matters, are arrested.

Conglomerate. A rock consisting of fragments of other rocks (usually rounded) cemented together.

Consume. The chemical and mechanical loss of mercury in amalgamation.

Contact. The plane between two adjacent bodies of dissimilar rock. A *contact-vein* is a vein, and a *contact-bed* is a bed, lying, the former more or less closely, the latter absolutely, along a contact.

Continental process. See German *process*.

Converter. See *Bessemer process*.

Cope. 1. DERB. To contract to mine lead-ore by the *dish*, load, or other measure. 2. The upper part of a *flask*, separable from the lower part. See *Drag*.

Coper, DERB. One who contracts to raise lead-ore at a fixed rate.

Copperas. Ferrous sulphate.

Copper-ores. Native copper; red copper-ore (*cuprite*, protoxide); green and blue *malachite* (*malachite* and *azurite*, carbonates); *copper glance* (*chalcocite*, sulphide); *purple copper* (variegated or *peacock* ore, *bornite*, sulphide of copper and iron); *gray copper* (*fahl-ore*, *tetrahedrite*, sulphantimonide of copper and other metals); *yellow copper* (*copper-pyrites*, *chalcopyrite*, sulphide of copper and iron); *copper-lead ore* (*bournonite*, sulphantimonide of lead and copper); *black copper-ore* (an earthy and variable mixture of sulphide and oxide of copper).

Copper-plates, AUSTR. and PAC. The plates of amalgamated copper over which the auriferous ore is allowed to flow from the stamp battery, and upon which the gold is caught as amalgam.

Copper-rain. Minute globules thrown up from the surface of molten copper, when it contains but little suboxide.

Copper-smoke. The gases from the calcination of sulphuretted copper-ores.

Corbond. An irregular mass or "dropper" from a lode.

Cordurié process. The refining of lead by conducting steam through it, while molten, to oxidize certain metallic impurities.

Core, CORN. A miner's underground working-time or *shift.*

Corf, Corve, or *Couf* (the last incorrect). 1. NEWC. A large basket used in hoisting coal; from the GERM. *Korb.* 2. A wooden frame to carry coal. 3. A sled or low wagon for the same purpose.

Cornish pump. A pump operated by rods attached to the beam of a single-acting, condensing beam-engine. The steam, pressing down the piston in the vertical steam-cylinder, lifts the pump-rods, and these subsequently descend by their own weight.

Coro-coro. A dressed product of copper-works in South America, consisting of grains of native copper mixed with pyrite, chalco-pyrite, mispickel, and earthy minerals.

Corroding-lead. Refined lead, sufficiently pure for the corroding process, by which white lead is manufactured.

Cost-book, CORN. A book used to keep accounts of mining enterprises carried on under the *cost-book system,* peculiar to Cornwall and Devon, and differing from both partnership and incorporation. It resembles the mining partnership system of the Pacific States.

Costeaning or *Costeening,* CORN. Discovering veins by pits and open cuts, run on the surface transversely to the supposed course of the veins.

Counter. 1. A cross-vein. 2. (Or *counter-gangway.*) A gangway driven obliquely upwards on a coal-seam from the main gangway until it cuts off the faces of the workings, and then continues parallel with the main gangway. The oblique portion is called the *run.*

Country, or *country-rock,* CORN. The rock traversed by or adjacent to an ore deposit.

Course. See *Strike.*

Course of ore. See *Chute* (2.).

Coursing. Conducting the air-current of a mine in different directions by means of doors and stoppings.

Cousin Jack. A common nickname for a Cornishman.

Covered-binding, CORN. See *Plank-timbering*.

Cow. A kind of self-acting brake for inclined planes; a trailer.

Cowl. See *Water-barrel*.

Cowper-Siemens stove. A hot-blast stove of firebrick on the regenerative-principle.

Coyoting, PAC. Mining in irregular openings or burrows, comparable to the holes of *coyotes* or prairie foxes.

Crab. A machine for moving heavy weights. Specially the engines employed for lowering into place the pumps, rods, pipes, etc., of Cornish *pit-work*.

Cradle, PAC. See *Rocker*.

Cramp. A pillar of rock or mineral left for support.

Cranch. Part of a vein left by old workers.

Craze or *Creuze*, CORN. The tin-ore which collects in the middle part of the *buddle*.

Creep, NEWC. A rising of the floor of a gangway, occasioned by the weight of incumbent strata, in pillar workings. Also any slow movement of mining ground.

Cretaceous. 1. Chalky. 2. See *Geological formations*.

Crevet. A crucible.

Crevice, PAC. 1. A shallow fissure in the bed-rock under a gold placer, in which small but highly concentrated deposits of gold are found. 2. The fissure containing a vein.

Crib. 1. See *Curb*. 2. A structure composed of frames of timber laid horizontally upon one another, or of timbers built up as in the walls of a log-cabin. 3. A miner's luncheon.

Cribbing. Close timbering, as the lining of a shaft, or the construction of *cribs* of timber or timber and earth or rock, to support a roof.

Cribble. A sieve.

Crop. 1. CORN. See *Crop-tin*. 2. The *basset* or outcrop of strata at the surface. 3. To leave coal at the bottom of a bed.

Cropping out. The rising of layers of rock to the surface. That part of a vein which appears above the surface is called the *cropping* or *outcrop*.

Crop-tin. The chief portion of tin-ore separated from waste in the principal dressing operation.

Cross-course, CORN. An intersecting (usually a barren) vein.

Cross-cut. A level driven across the course of a vein, or, in general, across the direction of the main workings (as to connect two parallel gangways), or across the "grain of coal."

Cross-heading. A heading driven across from one gangway or breast to another, usually for ventilation.

Cross-vein. An intersecting vein.

Crow or *crow-foot.* A tool with a side-claw, for grasping and recovering broken rods in deep bore-holes.

Crucible. 1. A melting pot. 2. The lower part of a shaft furnace, in which fusion is effected and the molten bath is contained.

Crush. 1. A squeeze, accompanied, perhaps, with more violent motion and effects. 2. A variety of fault in coal. See *Fault* (2).

Crusher. A machine for crushing ores.

Cry of tin. The peculiar crackling noise produced in bending a piece of metallic tin.

Culm. 1. ENG. Anthracite. 2. PENN. The waste or *slack* of the Pennsylvania anthracite mines, consisting of fine coal, more or less pure, and coal-dust and dirt.

Cup-and-cone. A machine for charging a shaft-furnace, consisting of an iron hopper with a large central opening, which is closed by a *cone* or *bell,* pulled up into it from below. In the annular space around this cone, the ore, fuel, etc., are placed; then the cone is lowered to drop the materials into the furnace; after which it is again raised to close the hole.

Cupellation. The treatment on a hearth or *cupel* (usually formed of bone-ash) of an alloy of lead, gold, and silver, by means of fusion and an air blast, which oxidizes the lead to litharge, and removes it in liquid form, or absorbs it in the cupel.

Cupola. A shaft-furnace with a blast, for remelting metals, preparatory to casting. Sometimes incorrectly pronounced and written *Cupalo.*

Curb. A timber frame, circular or square, wedged in a shaft to make a foundation for walling or tubbing, or to support, with or without other timbering, the walls of the shaft.

Curbing. See *Cribbing.*

Cut. 1. To intersect a vein or working. 2. To excavate coal.

Dam. 1. To keep back water in a stream or mine by means of a dam or bulkhead. 2. S. STAFF. See *Stopping* and *Bulkhead.* 3. The wall of refractory material, forming the front of the *fore-hearth* of a blast furnace. It is built on the inside of a supporting iron plate (*dam-plate*). Iron is tapped through a hole in the dam, and cinder through a notch in the top of the dam. See *Lürmann front.*

Damask. The etched or "watered" surface produced on polished (welded) steel by corrosion.

Damper. A valve in a flue or at the top of a chimney to regulate the draft.

Dam-plate. The plate upon the *dam-stone* or front stone of the bottom of a blast furnace.

Damp sheet, S. STAFF. A large sheet, placed as a curtain or partition across a gate-road to stop and turn an air-current.

Dan, NEWC. A truck or sled used in coal mines.

Danks puddler. A revolving mechanical puddler. See *Puddling.*

Dant, NEWC. Soft, inferior coal; *mineral charcoal.*

Davy lamp. The safety lamp invented by Sir H. Davy.

Day, WALES. The surface of the ground over a mine. *Day-level.* An *adit. Day-water.* Water from the surface.

Dead, CORN. 1. Unventilated. 2. As to a vein or piece of ground, unproductive.

Deadened mercury. See *Floured.*

Dead-plate. A nearly horizontal iron plate, at the mouth of the furnace, under a steam-boiler, on which the bituminous coal charges are laid to be partially coked before they are pushed upon the grate where their solid carbon is consumed. The gases evolved on the *dead-plate* pass over the grate and are burned.

Dead riches. See *Base bullion.*

Dead roasting. Roasting carried to the farthest practicable degree in the expulsion of sulphur.

Deads, CORN. The waste rock, packed in excavations from which ore or coal has been extracted.

Dead-work. Work that is not directly productive, though it may be necessary for exploration and future production.

Deal. Plank used in shaft and gallery construction.

Dean, CORN. The end of a level.

Débris, FR. The fragments resulting from shattering or disintegration.

Deep, CORN. The lower portion of a vein; used in the phrase *to the deep, i. e.,* downward upon the vein.

Denunciar, SP. To denounce. To give information that a mine is forfeited for being insufficiently worked, or for a violation of some condition which imposes that penalty. This term is also applied to the giving notice of a discovery, for the purpose of registry.

Deposit. The term *mineral deposit* or *ore-deposit* is arbitrarily used to designate a natural occurrence of a useful mineral or ore in extent and degree of concentration to invite exploitation.

Derrick. 1. See *Whip.* 2. The hoisting-tower over an artesian well-boring.

Descension-theory. The theory that the material in veins entered from above.

Desilverization. The process of separating silver from its alloys.

Desuing, CORN. See *Dissuing.*

Desulphurization. The removal of sulphur from sulphuret ores.

Dial, CORN. See *Compass.* To *dial* a mine is to make a survey of it.

Diamond-drill. A form of rock-drill in which the work is done by abrasion instead of percussion, black diamonds (*borts*) being set in the head of the boring tool.

Diamond groove. A groove of V-section in a *roll.*

Die. A piece of hard iron, placed in a mortar to receive the blow of a stamp, or in a pan to receive the friction of the muller. Between the die and the stamp or muller the ore is crushed.

Dig, CORN. See *Gouge.*

Diggings. Applicable to all mineral deposits and mining camps, but in usage in the United States applied to placer-mining only.

Dike. A vein of igneous rock.

Dilluing or *dilleughing,* CORN. An operation performed in tin-dressing upon the slimes of a certain part of the process. It is like the operation of *panning,* only performed with a sieve having a close haircloth bottom, and in a *kieve* of water which receives the tailings of the process.

Diluvium. Sand, gravel, clay, etc., in superficial deposits. See *Drift.* According to some authors, alluvium is the effect of the ordinary, and diluvium of the extraordinary action of water. The latter term is now passing out of use as not precise, and more specific names for the different kinds of material are substituted.

Dinas brick. A refractory brick, almost entirely composed of silica from the Dinas "clay" in the Vale of Neath, England.

Dip. The inclination of a vein or stratum below the horizontal. The dip at any point is necessarily at right angles with the local *strike,* and its inclination is steeper than that of any other line drawn in the plane of the vein or stratum through that point.

Dipping-needle. See *Compass.*

Discovery, PAC. The first finding of the mineral deposit in place upon a mining claim. A *discovery* is necessary before the location can be held by a valid title. The opening in which it is made is called *discovery-shaft, discovery-tunnel*, etc.

Dish, CORN. 1. The landowner's or landlord's part of the ore. 2. DERB. A measure of 14, 15, or 16 pints.

Dissuing, CORN. Cutting out the *selvage* or *gouge* of a lode, to facilitate the ore-extraction.

Distillation. Volatilization, followed by condensation to the liquid state.

District. In the States and Territories west of the Missouri, a vaguely bounded and temporary division and organization made by the inhabitants of a mining region. A district has one code of mining laws, and one recorder. Counties and county officers are gradually taking the place of these cruder arrangements.

Ditch. An artificial watercourse, flume, or canal, to convey water for mining. A flume is usually of wood; a ditch, of earth.

Divining-rod or *Dowsing-rod*, CORN. A rod (most frequently of witch-hazel, and forked in shape) used, according to an old but still extant superstition, for discovering mineral veins and springs of water, and even for locating oil wells.

Doggy, S. STAFF. An underground superintendent, employed by the *butty*.

Dog-hole.. A small *proving-hole* or airway, usually less than 5 feet high.

Dole. A division of a parcel of ore.

Dolly-tub, CORN. A tub in which ore is washed, being agitated by a *dolly*, or perforated board.

Dope. See *Explosives*.

Dotts or *Dott-holes*. Small openings in the vein.

Douglas process. See *Hunt and Douglas process*.

Downcast. The opening through which the ventilating air-current descends into a mine.

Downcome. The pipe through which *tunnel-head* gases from iron blast-furnaces are brought down to the hot-blast stoves and boilers, when these are below the *tunnel-head*.

Dradge, CORN. The inferior portions of ore, separated from the *prill* by cobbing.

Drag. The lower part of a *flask*. The mould having been prepared in the two parts of the flask, the *cope* is put upon the *drag* before casting. After casting, the flask is opened by removing the *cope*.

Drag-twist. A spiral hook at the end of a rod, for cleaning bore-holes.

Draught, S. STAFF. The quantity of coal raised *to bank* in a given time.

Draw. To *rob* pillars or the top-coal of breasts before abandoning the ground.

Dredge. Very fine mineral matter held in suspension in water.

Dresser, S. STAFF. A large pick, with which the largest lumps of coal are prepared for loading into the *skip.*

Dressing, CORN. The picking and sorting of ores, and washing, preparatory to reduction.

Drift. 1. A horizontal passage underground. A *drift* follows the vein, as distinguished from a *cross-cut,* which intersects it, or a *level* or *gallery,* which may do either. 2. Unstratified *diluvium.*

Drill. A metallic tool for boring in hard material. The ordinary miner's drill is a bar of steel, with a chisel-shaped end, and is struck with a hammer. See *Rock-drill, Diamond-drill.*

Driving. Extending excavations horizontally. Distinguished from *sinking* and *raising.*

Dropper, CORN. A branch leaving the main vein on the *footwall* side.

Dross. The material skimmed from the surface of freshly melted, not perfectly pure metal.

Drowned level. See *Blind level,* (2).

Druggon, S. STAFF. A square iron or wooden box, used for conveying fresh water for horses, etc., in a mine.

Drum. That part of the winding machinery on which the rope or chain is coiled.

Druse. A crystallized crust lining the sides of a cavity.

Dry, CORN. See *Changing-house.*

Dry copper. See *Under-poled copper.* Also copper just ready for poling.

Dry Puddling. See *Puddling.*

Dry sand. Sand prepared for *moulds* by thorough drying and baking. When special cohesion is required) as for *cores*) other substances, such as flour, molasses, etc., are mixed with it.

Dualin. See *Explosives.*

Dumb-drift. An *air-way* conveying air around, not through, a ventilating furnace to the *upcast.*

Dump. 1. To unload a vehicle by tilting or otherwise, without handling or shovelling out its contents. 2. A pile of ore or rock.

Dumper. A tilting-car used on *dumps.*
Durn, CORN. A frame of timbering, like a door-frame.
Dust-plate. A vertical iron plate, supporting the *slag-runner* of an iron blast furnace.
Dutch metal. An alloy of copper and zinc, containing more copper than ordinary brass.
Duty. A measure of the effectiveness of a steam-engine, usually expressed in the number of foot-pounds (or kilogrammetres) of useful work obtained from a given quantity of fuel.
Duty-ore, CORN. The landlord's share of the ore.
Dyke. See *Dike.*
Dzhu, CORN. To cut ahead on one side of a *face,* so as to increase the efficacy of blasting on the remainder. (Doubtless the same word as *Dissue.* See *Dissuing.*) Also called *to hulk.*

Egg-coal, PENN. See *Coal.*
Egg-hole, DERB. A notch cut in the wall of a lode to hold the end of a *stempel.*
Electrum. An alloy of copper, zinc, and nickel.
Eliquation. Separating an alloy by heating it so as to melt the more fusible of its ingredients, but not the less fusible.
Elutriation. Purification by washing and pouring off the lighter matter suspended in water, leaving the heavier portions behind.
Elvan, CORN. A name given to certain broad granite veins or belts in schistose rocks.
Emery. Impure corundum.
End of coal. The direction or section at right-angles to the *face ;* sometimes called the *butt.*
End-pieces, CORN. See *Wall-plates.*
English process. In copper-smelting, the process of *reduction* in a reverberatory furnace, after *roasting,* if necessary.
English zinc-furnace. A furnace in which zinc is reduced and distilled from *calcined* ores in *crucibles.*
Engorgement. The *clogging* of a furnace. See *Scaffold.*
Entry. An *adit.* Applied to the main *gangway* in some coal mines.
Estufa amalgamation, SP. A modification of the *patio* process, using heat.
Exploder. A cap or fulminating cartridge, placed in a charge of gunpowder or other explosive, and exploded by electricity or by a fuse. See *Explosives.*

Exploitation, FR. The productive working of a mine, as distinguished from exploration.

Explosives. The principal explosives used in mining are *gunpowder*, a compound of sulphur, charcoal, and potassium nitrate (potash saltpetre) or sodium nitrate (Chili or soda-saltpetre); *nitroglycerin*, a liquid compound of carbon, hydrogen, nitrogen, and oxygen, produced by the action of nitric acid upon glycerin; *dynamite No.* 1, or *giant-powder*, a mixture of nitroglycerin with a dry pulverized mineral or vegetable absorbent or *dope* (commonly silicious or infusorial earth); *dynamite No.* 2, nitroglycerin mixed with saltpetre, sawdust, or coaldust, paraffin, etc., in lieu of an inexplosive *dope; lithofracteur*, nitroglycerin mixed with silicious earth, charcoal, sodium (and sometimes barium) nitrate and sulphur; *dualin*, nitroglycerin, mixed with potassium nitrate and fine sawdust; *rend-rock, Hercules, Neptune, tonite, vigorite,* and other powders, resembling dynamite No. 2, *i. e.,* consisting of nitroglycerin with a more or less explosive *dope;* and *mica-powder,* a No. 1 *dynamite*, in which the *dope* is fine scales of mica. The *chlorate, picrate,* and *fulminate* explosives are not used in mining, except the fulminate of mercury, which is employed for the *caps* or *exploders*, by means of which charges of powder, dynamite, etc., are fired.

Eye. 1. The top of a shaft. 2. The opening at the end of a *tuyere,* opposite the *nozzle.* 3. The hole in a *pick* or hammer-head which receives the handle.

Face. 1. In any adit, tunnel, or stope, the end at which work is progressing or was last done. 2. The *face of coal* is the principal cleavage-plane at right angles to the stratification. Driving *on the face* is driving against or at right angles with the face.

Fagot. See *Pile.*

Fahlband, GERM. A zone or stratum in crystalline rock, impregnated with metallic sulphides. Intersecting fissure-veins are enriched by the *fahlband.*

Famp, N..WC. Soft, tough, thin shale beds.

Fan. A revolving machine, to blow air into a mine (*pressure-fan, blower*), or to draw it out (*suction-fan*).

Fanega, SP. A bushel; sometimes half a mule-load.

Fang, DERB. An air-course cut in the side of a shaft or level, or constructed of wood.

Fast-end. 1. The part of the coal-bed next the rock. 2. A gangway with rock on both sides. See *Loose-end.*

Fast shot, NEWC. A charge of powder exploding without the desired effect.

Fathom, CORN. Six feet. *A fathom of mining ground* is six feet square by the whole thickness of the vein, or in Cornish phrase, *a fathom forward by a fathom vertical.*

Fauld. The *tymp-arch* or working-arch of a furnace.

Fathom-tale, CORN. See *Tut-work* (2). This name probably arises from the payment for such work by the space excavated, and not by the ore produced.

Fault. 1. A dislocation of the strata or the vein. 2. In coal-seams, sometimes applied to the coal rendered worthless by its condition in the seam (*slate-fault, dirt-fault,* etc.).

Feather. See *Plug and feather.*

Feathered-shot. Copper granulated by pouring into cold water.

Feathering. See *Plugging.*

Feeder. 1. A small vein joining a larger vein. 2. A spring or stream. 3. A *blower* of gas.

Feigh, NEWC. Refuse washed from lead-ore or coal.

Feldspathic. Containing feldspar as a principal ingredient.

Fell. See *Riddle.*

Ferrie furnace. A high iron blast furnace, in the upper part of which crude bituminous coal is converted into coke.

Ferromanganese. An alloy of iron and manganese.

Ferruginous. Containing iron.

Fettle, Fettling. See *Fix.*

Fillet. The rounded corner of a *groove* in a *roll.*

Fin. The thin sheet of metal squeezed out between the collars of the *rolls* in a *roll-train.*

Fine metal. 1. See *Metal.* 2. The iron or plate-metal produced in the *refinery.*

Finery. A charcoal-hearth for the conversion of cast into malleable iron.

Fining. 1. See *Refining.* 2. The conversion of cast into malleable iron in a hearth or charcoal-fire.

Finishing-rolls. The *rolls* of a *train* which receive the bar from the *roughing-rolls,* and reduce it to its finished shape.

Fire-bars. Grate-bars in a fireplace.

Fire-bricks. Refractory bricks of fire-clay or of silicious material used to line furnaces.

Fire-bridge. The separating low wall between the fire-place and the *hearth* of a reverberatory furnace.

Fire-clay. A clay comparatively free from iron and alkalies, not easily fusible, and hence used for fire-bricks. It is often found beneath coal-beds.

Fire-damp. Light carburetted hydrogen gas. When present in common air to the extent of one-fifteenth to one-thirteenth by volume, the mixture is explosive.

Fire-setting. The softening or cracking of the working-face of a lode, to facilitate excavation, by exposing it to the action of a wood-fire built close against it. Now nearly obsolete, but much used in hard rock before the introduction of explosives.

Fire-stink, S. STAFF. The stench from decomposing iron pyrites, caused by the formation of sulphuretted hydrogen.

Fissure-vein. A fissure in the earth's crust filled with mineral.

Fix. To *fettle* or line with a *fix* or *fettling*, consisting of ores, scrap and cinder, or other suitable substances, the hearth of a puddling furnace.

Flang, CORN. A two-pointed miner's pick.

Flange. Applied to a vein widening.

Flap-door, NEWC. A manhole door.

Flask. 1. The wooden or iron frame which holds the sand-mould used in a foundry. 2. An iron bottle in which quicksilver is sent to market. It contains $76\frac{1}{2}$ pounds.

Flat, DERB. and N. WALES. A horizontal vein or ore-deposit auxiliary to a main vein; also any horizontal portion of a vein elsewhere not horizontal.

Flat-nose shell. A cylindrical tool with valve at bottom, for boring through soft clay.

Flat-rods. A series of horizontal or inclined connecting-rods, running upon rollers, or supported at their joints by rocking-arms, to convey motion from a steam-engine or water-wheel to pump-rods at a distance.

Flat-wall, CORN. A local term (in St. Just) for *foot-wall*.

Flintshire furnace. A *reverberatory* with a depression, *well* or *crucible* in the middle of the side of the hearth; used for the *roasting and reaction process* on lead ores.

Float-copper, LAKE SUP. Fine scales of metallic copper (especially produced by abrasion in stamping) which do not readily settle in water.

Float-gold, PAC. Fine particles of gold, which do not readily settle in water, and hence are liable to be lost in the ordinary stamp-mill process.

Float-ore. Water-worn particles of ore; fragments of vein-material found on the surface, away from the vein-outcrop.

Flookan or *Flooking,* CORN. See *Fluccan.*

Floor. 1. The rock underlying a stratified or nearly horizontal deposit, corresponding to the *foot-wall* of more steeply-dipping deposits. 2. A horizontal, flat ore-body. 3. A floor, in the ordinary sense, or a plank platform underground.

Floran-tin, CORN. Tin ore scarcely visible in the stone, or stamped very small.

Flosh, CORN. A rude mortar, with a shutter instead of a screen, used under stamps.

Floss. Fluid, vitreous cinder, floating in a puddling furnace.

Floss-hole. A tap-hole.

Floured. The finely granulated condition of quicksilver, produced to a greater or less extent by its agitation during the amalgamation process.

Flowing furnace. A *reverberatory* with inclined hearth, used in Cornwall for treating roasted lead ores by the *precipitation process.*

Fluccan, CORN. Soft clayey matter in the vein; a vein or course of clay.

Flue. A passage for air, gas, or smoke.

Flue-bridge. The separating low wall between the flues and the laboratory of a reverberatory furnace.

Flue-cinder. Iron-cinder from the reheating furnace, so called because it runs out from the lower part of the flue.

Flume. A wooden conduit, bringing water to a mill or mine.

Flux. A salt or other mineral, added in smelting to assist fusion, by forming more fusible compounds.

Foal, NEWC. A young boy employed in *putting* coal.

Fodder, NORTH ENG. A unit employed in expressing weights of metallic lead, and equal to 21 hundredweight of 112 pounds avoirdupois.

Foge, CORN. A forge for smelting tin.

Fondon. A large copper vessel, in which hot amalgamation is practiced.

Foot-piece. See *Sill.*

Foot-wall, CORN. The wall under the vein.

Foot-way. The series of ladders and *sollars* by which men enter or leave a mine.

Forefield, NEWC. The face of the workings. The *forefield-end* is the end of the workings farthest advanced.

Fore-hearth. A projecting bay in the front of a blast-furnace hearth, under the *tymp.* In *open-front* furnaces it is from the fore-hearth that cinder is tapped. See *Dam* and *Tymp.*

Forfeiture. The loss of possessory title to a mine or public lands by failure to comply with the laws prescribing the quantity of *assessment* work, or by actual abandonment.

Fore-poling. A method of securing drifts in progress through quicksand by driving ahead poles, lath, boards, slabs, etc., to prevent the inflow of the quicksand on the sides and top, the face being protected by *breast-boards.*

Forespar. See *Bloomary.*

Fore-winning, NEWC. Advanced workings.

Forge. 1. An open or semi-open *hearth* with a *tuyere.* 2. ENG. That part of an ironworks where *balls* are squeezed and hammered and then drawn out into *puddle-bars* by grooved rolls.

Forge-cinder. The slag from a forge or bloomary.

Formation. See *Geological formations.*

Fork. 1. CORN. The bottom of the *sump.* 2. DERB. A piece of wood supporting the side of an excavation in soft ground.

Forpale or *Forepale.* The driving of timbers or planks horizontally ahead at the working-face, to prevent the caving of the ground in subsequent driving.

Fossil ore. Fossiliferous red hematite.

Fother, NEWC. One-third of a chaldron.

Foundershaft. The first shaft sunk.

Fox-tail, S. WALES. The last cinder obtained in the *fining* process.

Frame, CORN. See *Tin-frame.*

Free. Native, uncombined with other substances, as free gold or silver.

Free fall. An arrangement by which, in deep boring, the *bit* is allowed to fall freely to the bottom at each drop or down-stroke.

Free-milling. Applied to ores which contain free gold or silver, and can be reduced by crushing and amalgamation, without roasting or other chemical treatment.

Freiberg amalgamation. See *Barrel amalgamation.*

Fritting. The formation of a slag by heat with but incipient fusion.

Frontal hammer or *Frontal helve*, ENG. A forge-hammer lifted by a cam, acting upon a "tongue" immediately in front of the hammer-head.

Frue ranner. A variety of continuously working *percussion-table.*

Fulguration. See *Blick.*

Furgen. A round rod used for sounding a bloomary fire.

Furnace. 1. A structure in which heat is produced by the combustion of fuel. 2. A structure in which, with the aid of heat so produced, the operations of roasting, reduction, fusion, steam-generation, desiccation, etc., are carried on, or, as in some mines, the *upcast* air-current is heated, to facilitate its ascent and thus aid ventilation.

Furnace cadmium or *cadmia.* The oxide of zinc which accumulates in the chimneys of furnaces smelting zinciferous ores.

Furtherance, NEWC. An extra price paid to *hewers* when they also *put* the coal.

Fuse. A tube or casing filled with combustible material, by means of which a blast is ignited and exploded.

Gad. 1. A steel wedge. 2. A small iron punch with a wooden handle used to break up ore.

Galemador, SP. A small Mexican furnace for roasting silver ores.

Gale, ENG. (Forest of Dean.) A grant of mining ground.

Galiage. Royalty.

Gallery. A level or drift.

Gallery-furnace. A retort-furnace used in the distillation of mercury.

Gallows-frame. A frame over a shaft, carrying the pulleys for the hoisting cables.

Galvanize. To coat with zinc.

Ganister. A mixture of ground quartz and fire-clay, used in lining Bessemer converters.

Gang. 1. A mine. 2. A set of miners.

Gangue. The mineral associated with the ore in a vein.

Gangway. 1. A main level, applied chiefly to coal mines. 2. NEWC. A wooden bridge.

Garland, S. STAFF. A trough or gutter round the inside of a shaft to catch the water running down the sides.

Gas-coal. See *Coal.*

Gas-furnace. A furnace employing gaseous fuel.

Gash. Applied to a vein wide above, narrow below, and terminating in depth within the formation it traverses.

Gas-producer. A furnace in which combustible gas is produced, to be used as fuel in another furnace.

Gas-well. A deep boring, from which natural gas is discharged.

Gate, Gate-way, or *Gate-road,* ENG. 1. A road or way underground for air, water, or general passage; a *gangway.* 2. The aperture in a founder's mould, through which the molten iron enters.

Gear, NEWC. 1. The working tools of a miner. 2. The mechanical arrangements connecting a motor with its work.

Geode. A cavity, studded around with crystals or mineral matter, or a rounded stone containing such a cavity.

Geological formations. Groups of rocks of similar character and age are called formations. The different stratified formations have been arranged by geologists according to their apparent age or order of position stratigraphically, and the fossils they contain. While there are minor points of difference in classification, and still more in nomenclature, the general scheme is now well settled. Three tables are given below, the first prepared in 1878, by Professor J. D. Dana, the second by Professor T. Sterry Hunt, both for the United States, and the third, referring to formations found in Pennsylvania only, by Professor J. P. Lesley. They are taken (Professor Hunt's, with later revision by the author), from *The Geologist's Travelling Handbook,* prepared by James Macfarlane, Ph.D. The numbers attached to the different formations in these tables will facilitate the identification of a given formation under different names. A catalogue of the formations is added to the tables, in which the predominant rocks of each are named. The eruptive rocks are not included in these tables, the determination of their age being a more difficult and doubtful matter, the discussion of which cannot be undertaken in this place. For lack of space, also, the enumeration and description of the different species of rocks and minerals must be omitted, the reader being referred for such information to works on lithology and mineralogy. (See next page.)

Geordie. The miners' term for Stephenson's safety-lamp.

German process. In copper smelting, the process of reduction in a *shaft-furnace,* after *roasting,* if necessary.

German silver. A white alloy of nickel, copper, and zinc.

German steel. See *Steel.*

Gerstenhöfer furnace. A *shaft-furnace* filled with terraces or shelves, through which crushed ore is caused to fall, for roasting.

Gig. See *Kibble.*

Gin. See *Whim.*

PROFESSOR J. D. DANA'S TABLE OF GEOLOGICAL FORMATIONS.

SYSTEMS OR AGES.	GROUPS OR PERIODS.	FORMATIONS OR EPOCHS.
Age of man.	20. Quaternary.	20. Quaternary.
Age of mammals.	19. Tertiary.	19 c. Pliocene. 19 b. Miocene. 19 a. Eocene.
Reptilian age.	18. Cretaceous.	18 c. Upper Cretaceous. 18 b. Middle Cretaceous. 18 a. Lower Cretaceous.
	17. Jurassic.	17. Jurassic.
	16. Triassic.	16. Triassic.
Carboniferous.	15. Permian.	15. Permian.
	14. Carboniferous.	14 c. Upper Coal Measures. 14 b. Lower Coal Measures. 14 a. Millstone Grit.
	13. Subcarboniferous.	13 b. Upper Subcarboniferous. 13 a. Lower Subcarboniferous.
Devonian or age of fishes.	12. Catskill.	12. Catskill.
	11. Chemung.	11 b. Chemung. 11 a. Portage.
	10. Hamilton	10 c. Genesee. 10 b. Hamilton. 10 a. Marcellus.
	9. Corniferous.	9 c. Corniferous. 9 b. Schoharie. 9 a. Cauda Galli.
SILURIAN OR AGE OF INVERTEBRATES. — Upper Silurian.	8. Oriskany.	8. Oriskany.
	7. Lower Helderberg.	7. Lower Helderberg.
	6. Salina.	6. Salina.
	5. Niagara.	5 c. Niagara. 5 b. Clinton. 5 a. Medina.
Lower Silurian.	4. Trenton.	4 c. Cincinnati. 4 b. Utica. 4 a. Trenton.
	3. Canadian.	3 c. Chazy. 3 b. Quebec. 3 a. Calciferous.
	2. Primordial or Cambrian.	2 b. Potsdam. 2 a. Acadian.
	1. Archæan.	1 b. Huronian. 1 a. Laurentian.

PROFESSOR T. STERRY HUNT'S TABLE OF GEOLOGICAL FORMATIONS.

AGES.	GROUPS.	AMERICAN FORMATIONS.
Cenozoic.	20. Quaternary. 19. Tertiary.	20. Recent. 19 c. Pliocene. 19 b. Miocene. 19 a. Eocene.
Mesozoic.	18. Cretaceous. 17. Jurassic. 16. Triassic.	18. Cretaceous. 17. New Red Sandstone. 16. New Red Sandstone.
Paleozoic.	13–15. Carboniferous.	15. Permo-Carboniferous. 14. Coal Measures. 13 b. Mississippi (Carb. Limestone). 13 a. Waverley or Bonaventure.
	8–12. Erian or Devonian.	12. Catskill. 11. Chemung and Portage. 10. Hamilton (including Genesee and Marcellus). 9. Corniferous or Upper Helderb'g 8. Oriskany.
	5–7. Silurian.	7. Lower Helderberg. 6. Onondaga or Salina. 5 c. Niagara (including Guelph). 5 b. Clinton. 5 a. Medina. 5 a. Oneida.
	4. Upper Cambrian, Siluro-Cambrian, Ordovician, or Ordovian.	4 c. Loraine. 4 b. Utica. 4 a. Trenton.
	3. Middle Cambrian.	3 c. Chazy. 3 b. Levis (Tremadoc and Arenig). 3 a. Calciferous.
	2. Lower Cambrian.	2 e. Potsdam. 2 d. Sillery. 2 c. Acadian (Menevian). 2 b. Taconian. 2 a. Keweenian.
Eozoic.	1. Primary or Crystalline.	1 e Montalban. 1 d. Norian or Labrador.* 1 c. Huronian. 1 b. Arvonian. 1 a. Laurentian.

* Professor Hunt says there are many reasons for believing that the Norian may be older than the Arvonian and Huronian.

PROFESSOR J. P. LESLEY'S PROVISIONAL NOMENCLATURE OF THE SECOND GEOLOGICAL SURVEY OF PENNSYLVANIA.

	NAMES PROVISIONALLY ADOPTED.	Numbers used in first survey.
	20. Quaternary. 16. Triassic. 14 c. Upper Barren Measures. 14 c. Monongahela River Coal Series. 14 b. Lower Barren Measures. 14 b. Allegheny River Coal Series. 14 a. Pottsville Conglomerate.	XIII. XIII. XIII. XIII. XII.
Bernician.	13 b. Mauch Chunk Red Shale. (Umbral.) 13 a. Pocono Gray Sandstone. (Vespertine.)	XI. X.
Devonian.	12. Catskill Red Sandstone. (Ponent.) 11 b. Chemung. 11 a. Portage. 10 c. Genesee. 10 b. Hamilton. 10 a. Marcellus. 9. Upper Helderberg. 8. Oriskany.	IX. VIII. VIII. VIII. VIII. VIII. VIII. VII.
Silurian.	7. Lower Helderberg. (Lewistown Limestone.) 5 b. Clinton. 5 a. Medina. 5 a. Oneida.	VI. V. IV. IV.
Siluro-Cambrian.	4 c. Hudson River. 4 b. Utica. 4 a. Trenton. 3 a. Calciferous. 2 b. Potsdam.	III. III. II. II. I.
	1. Azoic.	

NOTES.—In the following notes Professor Hunt's classification is sufficiently followed to show the nature of the older groups which he distinguishes.

1a. *Laurentian.* Chiefly massive gneiss, reddish or grayish, sparingly micaceous, often hornblendic. Some crystalline limestone, magnetic iron, and other metallic ores.

1b. *Arvonian.* Chiefly petrosilex, often becoming quartziferous prophyry, with some quartzites and hornblendic rocks; magnetic and specular iron ores.

1c. *Norian.* Chiefly a feldspathic rock (norite), which sometimes carries garnet, epidote, etc.; also, great beds of titaniferous iron ore.

1d. *Huronian.* Chloritic schists, greenstone (diorite or dinbase), serpentine, steatite, dolomite, copper, chrome, nickel, and iron ores.

1e. *Montalban.* Fine-grained micaceous or hornblendic gneiss, chrysolite rock, serpentine, mica-schist, granite.

2a. *Keweenian.* The copper-bearing series of Lake Superior, made up of sandstones and conglomerates, with much interstratified eruptive rock.

2b. *Taconian.* Granular quartzites, argillites and nacreous or hydro-micaceous schists and great masses of crystalline limestone, marbles, magnetite, siderite, and pyrite changing to limonite.

2c and 2d. *Acadian* (and *Sillery*). Fossiliferous sandstone and shale.

2e. *Potsdam.* Sandstone, conglomerate.

3a. *Calciferous.* Sandy magnesian limestone, calcareous sandstone.
3b. *Quebec.* Sandstone, limestone conglomerate, black slate
3c. *Chazy.* Limestone, chert.
4a *Trenton.* Limestone, buff and blue; dolomite carrying lead ore deposits; brown-hematite beds.
4b. *Utica.* Dark carbonaceous slate; impure limestone.
4c. *Hudson River.* Slate, shale, clay, grit.
5a. *Medina.* Conglomerate; argillaceous sandstone.
5b. *Clinton.* Sandstone, shale, conglomerate, limestone, fossiliferous red hematite, or oolitic iron-ore bed.
5c. *Niagara.* Clay shale; limestone.
6. *Salina.* Red shale, gypseous shale, hydraulic lime, salt.
7. *Lower Helderberg.* Limestone, shaly or compact, and fossiliferous.
8. *Oriskany.* Sandstone.
9. *Corniferous or Upper Helderberg.* Principally limestone.
9a. *Cauda-galli.* Fine-grained calcareous and argillaceous, drab or brownish sandstone; peculiar fossils.
9b. *Schoharie Grit.* Fine-grained calcareous grit, similar to 9a, but with differing fossils.
9c. *Onondaga,* and 9d. *Corniferous.* Gray, blue, black limestone. At the top of 9d occur the Marcellus iron ores (carbonate).
10a. *Marcellus.* Black or dark-brown bituminous and pyritiferous shales. In 10a and 9d occur the petroleum deposits of Canada.
10b. *Hamilton.* Slate, shale, sandstone, calcareous and argillaceous.
10b. *Tully.* Impure dark limestone.
10c. *Genesee* Black clay slate.
11a. *Portage.* Green and black sandy and slaty shales, sandstone, flagstone.
11b. *Chemung.* Thin-bedded greenish sandstones and flagstones, with intervening shales, and rarely beds of impure limestone.
12. *Catskill.* Red, gray sandstone, grindstone grit, greenish shale, conglomerate.
13a. *Lower Subcarboniferous.* Sandstone, limestone, small local coal beds.
13b. *Upper Subcarboniferous.* Red shale, red and gray sandstone, blue limestone.
14a. *Millstone grit.* White or yellow sandstone, and conglomerate of quartz pebbles.
14b. and 14c. *Coal measures.* Fire-clay, shale, sandstone, conglomerate, limestone, bituminous coal, anthracite, iron ore, salt.
15. *Permian.* Limestone, sandstone, marl, shale.
16. *Triassic.* Red sandstone, red shale, conglomerate, lignite, trap dikes, copper ore, coal.
17. *Jurassic.* Marl, limestone, probably the gold-bearing slates of California.
18. *Cretaceous.* Earthy beds of sand, marl, clay, limestone, chalk, lignite.
19. *Tertiary.* Earthy sand, clay, marl, limestone, sandstone.
20. *Quaternary.* Sand, pebbles, boulders, clay, diluvium, alluvium; gravel and placer tin and gold deposits.

NOTE.—The primary and crystalline schistose rocks contain the larger number of mineral veins. The ancient magnesian limestones (probably Devonian) are characterized in many localities by deposits of argentiferous lead ore and of zinc ore.

Ginging, DERB. The lining of a shaft with masonry.
Giraffe. A car of peculiar construction to run on an incline.
Girdle. A thin bed of stone.
Girdle, NEWC. A thin stratum of stone.
Girth. In *square-set* timbering, a horizontal brace in the direction of the *drift*.
Glazy. See *Iron*.
Glist, CORN. Mica.
Glut, NEWC. A piece of wood, used to fill up behind *cribbing* or *tubbing*.
Goaf, ENG. An excavated space; also, the waste rock packed in old workings.
Goaves. Old workings.
Gob, S. WALES. See *Goaf*. Both terms are chiefly used in collieries, and are apparently the same word. Local usage seems to give to *goaf* rather the meaning of the space in which the roof has fallen after the *pillars* have been removed, and to *gob* that of a space packed with waste after *long-wall* extraction of the coal.
Gobbing. Packing with waste rock. See *Stowiny*.
Gob-up, ENG. Of a blast furnace, to become obstructed in working by reason of a *scaffold* or a *salamander*.
Gob-fire. Fire produced by the heat of decomposing *gob*.
Goffan or *Goffen*, CORN. A long narrow surface-working.
Gold-ores. Native gold; *telluric* gold ore (sylvanite, müllerite, nagyagite, tellurides of gold, silver, and lead); auriferous lead, zinc, and copper ores.
Good levels, CORN. Levels nearly horizontal.
Good roasting. See *Roasting*.
Gopher or *Gopher-drift.* An irregular prospecting-drift, following or seeking the ore without regard to maintenance of a regular grade or section.
Gossan or *Gozzan*, CORN. Hydrated oxide of iron, usually found at the decomposed outcrop of a mineral vein.
Gothic groove. A groove of Gothic arch section in a *roll*.
Gouge. A layer of soft material along the wall of a vein, favoring the miner, by enabling him after "gouging" it out with a pick, to attack the solid vein from the side.
Grain, ENG. Of coal, the lines of structure or parting parallel with the main gangways and hence crossing the *breasts*.
Grain-tin, CORN. 1. Crystalline tin ore. 2. Metallic tin.
Grapnel. An implement for removing the core left by an annu-

lar drill in a bore-hole, or for recovering tools, fragments, etc., fallen into the hole.

Grampus, U. S. The tongs with which *bloomary loups* and *billets* are handled.

Granzas, SP. Small pieces of ore.

Graphite. A crystalline form of carbon.

Graphitic carbon. That portion of the carbon in iron or steel which is present as graphite.

Grass, CORN. The surface over a mine. *Bringing ores to grass* is taking them out of the mine.

Grassero, SP. A slag-heap.

Grate, CORN. See *Screen* (as applied to stamps).

Grate coal, PENN. See *Coal*.

Gravel-mine, U. S. An accumulation of auriferous gravel.

Grueso, SP. Lump ore. The term is in use at the quicksilver mines of California.

Green sand. Sand used for moulds without previous drying or mixture.

Gray ore, CORN. Copper-glance. See *Copper-ores*.

Gray slag. The slag from the Flintshire lead furnace. It is rich in lead.

Griddle, CORN. A miner's sieve to separate ore from *halvans*.

Grip. A small, narrow cavity.

Grizzly, PAC. A grating to catch and throw out large stones from sluices.

Groove or *Grove*. 1. DERB. A mine; from the GERM. *Grube*. See *Roll*.

Ground, CORN. The rock in which a vein is found; also, any given portion of the mineral deposit itself.

Growan, CORN. Decomposed granite; sometimes the granite rock.

Gubbin. A kind of ironstone.

Grundy. Granulated pig iron.

Guard. A support in front of a *roll-train* to guide the bar into the groove, sometimes called a *side-guide*.

Guides. 1. The timbers at the side of a shaft to steady and guide the cage. 2. The holes in a cross-beam through which the stems of the stamps in a stamp-mill rise and fall. 3. In a rolling-mill a *guide* is a wedge-shaped piece held in the *groove* of a *roll* to prevent the sticking of the bar by peeling it out of the groove. When the guide is held by a hanger or counter-weight against the under side of the roll, it is called a *hanging-guide*.

Guillotine. A machine for breaking iron with a falling weight.
Gullet. An opening in the strata.
Gun-metal. An alloy of copper with tin or zinc, and sometimes a little iron. The common formula is nine parts copper to one tin. *Aich's metal* and some other gun-metals contain zinc and iron but no tin.
Gunnies or *Gunniss*, CORN. The vacant space left where the lode has been removed.

Hacienda, SP. Exchequer; treasury; public revenue; capital; funds; wealth; landed estate; establishment. In mining it is usually applied to the offices, principal buildings, and works for reducing the ores.
Hack. 1. See *Pick.* 2. A sharp blade on a long handle used for cutting billets in two.
Hade, DERB. See *Underlay.*
Hähner furnace. A continuously-working shaft furnace for roasting quicksilver ores. The fuel is charcoal, charged in alternate layers with the ore. The *Vall' Alta furnace* is a modification, having the iron tubes of the *Alberti.*
Hair-plate. See *Bloomary.*
Half-marrow, NEWC. Young boys, of whom two do the work of one *putter.*
Halvans, CORN. Ores much mixed with impurities.
Hammer-pick. See *Poll-pick.*
Hanging-coal. A portion of the coal-seam which, by the removal of another portion, has had its natural support removed, as in *holing.*
Hanging-guide. See *Guide.*
Hanging-side, or *Hanging-wall,* or *Hanger,* CORN. The wall or side over the vein.
Hazel. Freestone.
Hard head. A residual alloy, containing much iron and arsenic, produced in the refining of tin.
Hard lead. Lead containing certain impurities, principally antimony.
Hasenclever furnace. A roasting furnace, consisting of a long inclined channel (in its first form, a succession of inclined shelves in a shaft) down which the ore slides in a thin sheet, heated from below.
Head-gear. That part of deep-boring apparatus which remains at the surface.
Head-house. See *Gallows-frame.*
Heading. 1. The vein above a drift. See *Back.* 2. An interior

level or air-way driven in a mine. 3. In *long-wall* workings, a narrow passage driven upward from a gangway in starting a working in order to give a *loose end*.

Headings. In ore-dressing, the heavier portions collecting at the upper end of a buddle or sluice, as opposed to the *tailings*, which escape at the other end, and the *middlings*, which receive further treatment.

Head-piece. See *Cap.*

Headsman, NEWC. See *Putter.*

Head-stocks. See *Gallows-frame.*

Head-tree, NEWC. See *Cap.*

Headway, NEWC. See *Cross-heading.* The *headways* are the second set of excavations in *post-and-stall* work.

Heap, NEWC. The refuse at the pit's mouth.

Hearth. 1. The floor or *sole* of a reverberatory. 2. The *crucible* of a blast furnace.

Hearth-ends. Particles of unreduced lead ore expelled by the blast from a furnace.

Heat. One operation in a heating furnace, Bessemer *converter*, *puddling* furnace, or other furnace not operating continuously.

Heating-furnace. The furnace in which *blooms* or *piles* are heated before *hammering* or *rolling.*

Heave, CORN. A horizontal dislocation of a vein or stratum.

Helve. A *lift-hammer* for forging *blooms.*

Henderson process. The treatment of copper sulphide ores by roasting with salt, to form chlorides, which are then leached out and precipitated. Henderson originally proposed to volatilize the chlorides, and the leaching and precipitation are not original with him. *Longmaid* and many other metallurgists have proposed them in various modifications.

Hercules powder. See *Explosives.*

Hewer, NEWC. The man who *cuts* the coal.

Hitch, SCOT. and NEWC. 1. A minor dislocation of a vein or stratum not exceeding in extent the thickness of the vein or stratum. 2. A hole cut in the side-rock, when this is solid enough, to hold the *cap* of a set of timbers, permitting the *leg* to be dispensed with.

High explosive. An explosive or detonating compound developing more intense and instantaneous force than gunpowder. Most high explosives in general use contain nitroglycerin. See *Explosives.*

Hog-back. 1. A sharp anticlinal, decreasing in height at both ends until it runs out. 2. A ridge produced by highly tilted strata.

Hogger-pipe. The upper terminal pipe of the mining pump.

Hogger-pump. The topmost pump in a shaft.

Holing. 1. The working of a lower part of a bed of coal for bringing down the upper mass. 2. The final act of connecting two workings underground.

Hollow-fire, ENG. A kind of hearth with blast, used for reheating the *stamps* produced in the South Welsh process of fining, or the bars of *blister-steel* in the manufacture of *shear-steel.*

Hollway process. The removal of sulphur from iron and copper sulphides by fusion and pneumatic treatment, analogous to the manner in which carbon, etc., are removed in the Bessemer process.

Homogeneous metal. A variety of *ingot-metal* produced by the open-hearth process. See *Steel.*

Hopper. 1. A trap at the foot of a *shoot* for regulating the contents of a wagon. 2. A place of deposit for coal or ore.

Horn. See *Spoon.*

Horse, CORN. 1. A mass of *country-rock* inclosed in an ore-deposit. 2. See *Salamander.*

Horse-back, NEWC. A portion of the roof or floor which bulges or intrudes into the coal.

Horse-flesh ore, CORN. Bornite. See *Copper-ores.*

Horse-gin. Gearing for hoisting by horse-power.

Hot-bed. A platform in a rolling-mill on which rolled bars lie to cool.

Hot-blast. Air forced into a furnace after having been heated.

Hotching, NORTH ENG. See *Jigging.*

House of water, CORN. A cavity or space filled with water.

Howell furnace. A form of revolving roasting furnace.

H-piece. That part of a *plunger-lift* in which the valves or *clacks* are fixed.

Hudge. An iron bucket for hoisting ore or coal.

Hulk. See *Dzhu.*

Huel, CONN. See *Wheal.*

Hungry. A term applied to hard barren vein-matter, such as white quartz (not discolored with iron oxide).

Hunt & Douglas process. The treatment of copper oxide (or roasted sulphide) ores by dissolving the oxides of copper in a hot solution of protochloride of iron and common salt. From the solution thus obtained, metallic iron precipitates metallic copper, at the same time regenerating the protochloride of iron for further use.

Hurdy-gurdy wheel. A water-wheel operated by the direct impact of a stream upon its radially-placed paddles.

Hushing. The discovery of veins by the accumulation and sudden discharge of water, which washes away the surface soil and lays bare the rock. See *Booming.*

Hutch. 1, SCOT. A low car, suited both to run in a level and to be hoisted on a cage. 2, CORN. A cistern or box for washing ore. See *Jig.*

Hydraulicking, PAC. Washing down a bank of earth or gravel by the use of pipes, conveying water under high pressure.

Idria furnace. See *Leopoldi furnace.*

Impregnation. An ore-deposit consisting of the country-rock impregnated with ore, usually without definite boundaries.

Inbye or *Inbyeside,* NEWC. Further into a mine, away from the shaft.

Incline. 1. A shaft not vertical; usually on the dip of a vein. See *Slope.* 2. A *plane,* not necessarily under ground.

Indicator. 1. An instrument for showing at any moment the position of the cage in the shaft. 2. An instrument for recording, by a diagram, upon a card the varying pressure of the steam in the cylinder of a steam-engine during the stroke.

Infiltration-theory. The theory that a vein was filled by the infiltration of mineral solutions.

Ingot. A cast bar or block of metal.

Injection-theory. The theory that a vein was filled first with molten mineral.

In place. Of rock, occupying, relative to surrounding masses, the position that it had when formed.

Inquartation. See *Quartation.*

Intake. The passage by which the ventilating current enters a mine. See *Downcast,* which is more appropriate for a shaft; *Intake* for an adit.

Inwalls. The interior walls or lining of a *shaft-furnace.*

Irestone or *Ironstone,* CORN. Greenstone.

Irestone. Hard clay slate; hornstone; hornblende.

Iron. The principal varieties of iron are *wrought-iron* and *cast-iron* (see *Pig-iron*). *Wrought-iron,* also called *bar-iron* and *weld-iron,* is the product of the forge or the puddling furnace, *cast-iron* of the blast furnace. The former approaches pure iron; the latter is an alloy of iron and carbon. Steel (except some of the so-called "low"

50   A GLOSSARY OF MINING AND METALLURGICAL TERMS.

or "mild" steels, which are more nearly wrought-iron fused and cast) stands between them, having less carbon than cast-iron and more than wrought-iron. Some of the carbon in cast-iron is usually segregated during cooling in the form of graphite, and this determines the grade of the iron as *No.* 1 *foundry* (the most graphitic, coarsely crystalline, soft and black), *No.* 2 *foundry* (less open in grain), *gray forge* or *mill-iron* (still closer in grain, suitable for puddling), *mottled* (spotted with *white iron*), and *white* (hard, brittle, radially crystalline, containing its carbon mostly in alloy with the iron, and showing no visible graphite). These grades are also called simply No. 1, 2, 3, etc. So-called *silver-gray*, *glazy*, or *carbonized iron* is usually an iron rendered brittle by excess of silicon. *Ingot iron*, see *Steel*. *Anthracite, charcoal,* and *coke iron* are names given to pig-iron according to the fuel with which it is made.

Iron hat.   See *Gossan.*

Iron-ores: Magnetic (magnetite, protoperoxide), *specular (hematite* proper, *red hematite,* anhydrous peroxide), *brown iron ore (hematite, brown hematite, limonite,* etc., hydrated peroxides), *spathic (siderite,* carbonate), clay-ironstone (*black band,* argillaceous *siderite).*   See *Fossil ore.*

Iron-reduction process.   See *Precipitation process.*

Ironstone.   1. Iron-ore.   2. See *Irestone.*

Jacket.   A covering to prevent radiation of heat, as the jacket of a steam boiler ; also, a casing around a furnace hearth in which water is allowed to stand or circulate to keep the walls cool.

Jackhead-pit.   A small shaft sunk within a mine.

Jackhead-pump.   A subordinate pump in the bottom of a shaft, worked by an attachment to the main pump-rod.

Jack-roll, NEWC.   See *Windlass.*

Judding or *Judding.*   See *Holing.*

Jagging.   A mode of carrying ore to the reduction-works in bags on horses, mules, etc.

Jars.   A part of percussion-drilling apparatus for deep holes, which is placed between the *bit* and the *rods* or *cable,* and which by producing at each up-stroke a decided jar of the *bit* jerks it up, though it may be tightly wedged in the hole.

Jig-brow.   See *Jinny-road.*

Jig-chain.   S. STAFF.   A chain hooked to the back of a *skip* and running round a post, to prevent its too rapid descent on an inclined plane.

Jigging, CORN. Separating ores according to specific gravity with a sieve agitated up and down in water. The apparatus is called a *jig* or *jigger*.

Jinny-road. A gravity plane underground.

Joachimsthal process. The extraction of silver from sulphuretted ores by converting into chloride, leaching with sodium hyposulphite, and precipitating the silver as sulphide with sodium sulphide.

Jowl, NEWC. A noise made for a signal by hammering at the faces of two levels expected to meet.

Judge, DERB. and NEWC. A measuring-stick to measure coal-work under ground.

Judd, NEWC. In *whole working*, a portion of the coal laid out and ready for extraction; in *pillar-working* (i. e., the drawing or extraction of pillars), the yet unremoved portion of a pillar.

Jugglers. Timbers set obliquely against pillars of coal, to carry a plank partition, making a triangular air-passage or man-way.

Jump. 1, PAC. To take possession of a mining claim alleged to have been forfeited or abandoned. 2. A dislocation of a vein.

Jumper, CORN. and NEWC. A drill or boring tool, consisting of a bar, which is "jumped" up and down in the bore-hole.

Kann. See *Cand*.

Kast furnace. A small circular shaft furnace with three or four tuyeres, for lead smelting.

Keckle-meckle. The poorest kind of lead ore.

Keere. 1. See *Cauf*. 2. A tub used in collecting grains of heavy ore or metal; a dolly tub.

Kernel-roasting. See *Roasting*.

Keril, DERB. A veinstone, consisting of a mixture of carbonate of lime and other minerals.

Kibbal or *Kibble*, CORN. and WALES. An iron bucket for raising ore.

Kicker. Ground left in first cutting a vein, for support of its sides.

Kieve, CORN. A tub for *tozing* tin-ore.

Killas, CORN. Clay-slate.

Kiln. A furnace for the calcination of coarsely broken ore or stone; also, an oven for drying, charring, etc.

Kind's plug. A wooden plug attached to an iron rod, used in connection with sand for recovering *tubing* from *bore-holes*.

King-pot. The large central pot or crucible in a brass-melting furnace.

King's yellow. Sulphide of arsenic.

Kirving, NEWC. The cutting made at the bottom of the coal by the hewer.

Kish. The blast-furnacemen's name for the graphite-segregations seen in pig-iron and in the cinder of a furnace making a very gray iron.

Kit. A wooden vessel.

Kitchen. See *Laboratory* (2).

Knits or *Knots.* Small particles of ore.

Knobbling-fire. A bloomary for refining cast-iron.

Knockings. See *Riddle.*

Knox & Osborne furnace. A continuously working shaft-furnace for roasting quicksilver ores, having the fireplace built in the masonry at one side. The fuel is wood.

Knots. Small particles of ore.

Kröhnke process. The treatment of silver ores preparatory to amalgamation, by humid chloridization with copper dichloride.

Krupp washing process. The removal of silicon and phosphorus from molten pig iron by running it into a *Pernot furnace,* lined with iron oxides. Iron ore may also be added, and the bath is agitated by rotation for five to eight minutes only. See *Bell's dephosphorizing process.*

Labor, SP. Labor; work; a working. This term is applied in mining to the work which is actually going on, and to the spaces which have been dug out. It includes galleries, cavities, and shafts.

Laboratory. 1. A place fitted up for chemical analysis, etc. 2. The space between the fire and flue-bridges of a *reverberatory* furnace in which the work is performed; also called the *kitchen* and the *hearth.*

Ladle. A vessel into which molten metal is conveyed from the furnace or crucible, and from which it is poured into the moulds.

Lagging. Planks, slabs, or small timber placed over the caps or behind the posts of the timbering, not to carry the main weight, but to form a ceiling or a wall, preventing fragments of rock from falling through.

Lame-skirting, NEWC. Widening a passage by cutting coal from the side of it.

Lander, CORN. The man at the shaft-mouth who receives the *kibble*.

Landry-box, NEWC. A box at the top of a set of pumps into which the water is delivered.

Lath door-set. A weak lath-frame surrounding a main door-frame, the space between being for the insertion of *spills*.

Lath-frame or *crib*. A weak lath-frame, surrounding a main crib, the space between being for the insertion of *piles*.

Laths, CORN. The *boards* or *lagging* put behind the *durns*.

Launder, CORN. A wooden trough, gutter or sluice.

Lazadores, SP. Persons employed to collect workmen for a mine.

Lazyback, S. STAFF. The place at the surface where coal is stacked for sale.

Leaching. See *Lixiviation*.

Lead (pronounced like the verb *to lead*), PAC. See *Lode*.

Lead-fume. The fumes escaping from lead furnaces, and containing both volatilized and mechanically suspended metalliferous compounds.

Leader, CORN. A small vein leading to a larger one.

Lead-ores. Galena (*galenite*, sulphide); *antimonial lead-ore* (*bournonite*, sulphantimonide of lead and copper); *white lead-ore* (*cerussite*, carbonate); *green lead-ore* (*pyromorphite*, the phosphate, or *mimetite* or *mimetesite*, the arseno-chloride); *lead-vitriol* (*anglesite*, sulphate); *yellow lead-ore* (*wulfenite*, molybdate); *red lead-ore* (*crocoite*, chromate).

Lead-spar, CORN. Anglesite. See *Lead-ores*.

Leap, DERB. A fault. See *Jump*.

Leat, CORN. A watercourse.

Leath. Applied to the soft part of a vein.

Leavings, CORN. The ores left after the *crop* has been removed.

Ledge, PAC. See *Lode*.

Ledger-wall. See *Foot-wall*.

Leg. A prop of timber supporting the end of a *stull*, or the *cap* of a set of timber.

Leopoldi furnace. A furnace for roasting quicksilver ores, differing from the *Bustamente* in having a series of brick condensing chambers. Both are intermittent, *i. e.*, have to be charged and fired anew after each operation. The *California intermittent furnace* is a modification of the *Leopoldi*, having the fireplace on the side.

Level. A horizontal passage or drift into or in a mine. It is customary to work mines by levels at regular intervals in depth, numbered in their order below the adit or drainage level, if there be one.

Lewis. An iron instrument for raising heavy blocks of stone.

Ley, Sp. Proportion of metal in the ore; fineness of bullion; also, an alloy or base metal.

Lid. A flat piece of wood placed between the end of a *prop* or *stempel* and the rock.

Lifters, Corn. The wooden beams used as *stems* for stamps in old-fashioned stamp-mills.

Lift-hammer. See *Tilt-hammer.*

Lifting-dog. A claw-hook for grasping a column of bore-rods while raising or lowering them.

Lignite. See *Coal.*

Limp. An instrument for striking the refuse from the sieve in washing ores.

Lining, Newc. See *Dialling.*

Linnets, Derb. Oxidized lead-ores.

Liquation. See *Eliquation.*

Litharge. Protoxide of lead.

Lithofracteur. See *Explosives.*

Little Giant. A jointed iron nozzle used in hydraulic mining.

Lixiviation. The separation of a soluble from an insoluble material by means of washing with a solvent.

Location. 1. The act of fixing the boundaries of a mining claim, according to law. 2. The claim itself.

Loam. An impure potter's clay, containing mica or iron ochre.

Loch, Derb. and Wales. See *Vug.*

Lock-timber. An old plan of putting in *stull-pieces* in Cornwall and Devon. The pieces were called *lock-pieces.*

Lode, Corn. Strictly a fissure in the country-rock filled with mineral; usually applied to metalliferous lodes. In general miner's usage, a *lode, vein,* or *ledge* is a tabular deposit of valuable mineral between definite boundaries. Whether it be a fissure formation or not is not always known, and does not affect the legal title under the United States federal and local statutes and customs relative to lodes. But it must not be a placer, *i. e.,* it must consist of quartz or other rock *in place,* and bearing valuable mineral.

Lodge, Wales. See *Platt.*

Log, S. Staff. A balance-weight near the end of the hoisting-rope of a shaft to prevent its running back over the pulley.

Longmaid process. See *Henderson process.*

Long tom, Pac. A kind of gold-washing cradle.

Long-wall. A method of coal mining by which the whole seam is taken out as the working faces progress, and the roof is allowed to fall behind the workers, except where passages must be kept open, or where the *gob* being packed in the space formerly occupied by the coal, prevents caving. According as the work of extraction begins at the boundary of the *winning*, and converges back to the shaft, or begins with the coal nearest the shaft and proceeds outward to the boundaries, it is called *long-wall retreating* or *long-wall advancing.*

Loob or *loobs*, CORN. The clayey or slimy portion washed out of tin-ore in *dressing.*

Loop. See *Loup.*

Loop-dray. An eye at the end of a rod through which tow is passed for cleaning bore-holes.

Loose-end. A gangway in *long-wall* working, driven so that one side is solid ground while the other opens upon old workings. See *Fast-end.*

Lorry. A hand-car used on mine tramways.

Lost level, CORN. "Level" is "lost" when a gallery has been driven with an unnecessarily great departure from the horizontal.

Loup. The pasty mass of iron produced in a *bloomary* or puddling furnace. See *Puddle-ball.*

Lowe, NEWC. A light. A "piece of lowe" is part of a candle.

Luckhart furnace. A continuously working shaft-furnace for roasting quicksilver ores, having the fireplace in the shaft at the bottom, protected by a cast-iron roof. The fuel is wood.

Lum. A chimney over an upcast pit.

Lump-coal, PENN. See *Coal.*

Lürmann front. An arrangement of water-cooled castings through which iron and cinder are tapped from the blast furnace, thus avoiding the use of a forehearth. See *Closed front.*

Lying-wall. See *Foot-wall.*

Machine-whim. A rotary steam-engine for winding.

Magistral, SP. A powder of roasted copper pyrites, used in the amalgamation of silver ores.

Main-rod, CORN. See *Pump-rod.*

Mainway. A *gangway* or principal passage.

Makings, NEWC. The small coals hewn out in *kirving.*

Malleable castings. Small iron castings made malleable by "annealing" or decarburizing by cementation in powdered hematite or other oxide of iron.

Mallet, CORN. The sledge-hammer used for striking or *beating* the borer.

Mandril. See *Maundril.*

Manganese-ores. Gray oxide (*pyrolusite, polianite,* anhydrous peroxide, and *manganite,* hydrated sesquioxide); *black manganese* (*hausmannite,* protoperoxide); *braunite* (anhydrous sesquioxide); *red manganese ore* (*rhodochrosite,* a carbonate, or *rhodonite,* a silicate); also, manganiferous iron ores.

Man-hole, CORN. The hole in a *sollar* through which men pass upon the ladder or from one ladder to the next.

Man-machine or *Man-engine*, CORN and DERB. A mechanical lift for lowering and raising miners in a shaft by means of a reciprocating vertical rod of heavy timber with platforms at intervals, or of two such rods, moving in opposite directions. In the former case, stationary platforms are placed in the shaft, so that the miner in descending, for instance, can step from the moving platform at the end of the down-stroke, and step back upon the next platform below at the beginning of the next down-stroke. When two rods are employed, the miner steps from the platform on one rod to that on the other.

Man-of-war, STAFF. A small pillar of coal left in a critical spot; also, a principal support in thick coal workings.

Manta, SP. Blanket; sack of ore.

Mantle. The outer wall and casing of an iron *blast furnace,* above the *hearth.*

Manway. A small passage, used by workmen but not for transportation.

Maquilla, SP. A mill where ore is ground on shares.

Marl. Calcareous clay, sometimes used for the hearths of cupelling-furnaces.

Martin process. Called also the *Siemens-Martin* and the *open-hearth* process. See *Steel.*

Mass-copper, LAKE SUP. Native copper, occurring in large masses.

Massicot. See *Litharge.*

Matrix. The rock or earthy material containing a mineral or metallic ore; the *gangue.*

Matt, or *Matte,* FR. A mass consisting chiefly of metallic sulphides got in the fusion of ores.

Maul, DERB. A large hammer or mallet.

Maundril, DERB. and S. WALES. A prying *pick* with two prongs.

Mear. DERB. Thirty-two yards of ground measured on the vein.

Measures. Strata of coal, or the formation containing coal beds.

Meat-earth. The vegetable mould.

Meetings, NEWC. The place at middle-depth of a *shaft, slope*, or *plane*, where ascending and descending cars pass each other.

Merced, SP. A gift. This term is applied to a grant which is made without any valuable consideration.

Merchant-iron. See *Mill*.

Merchant-train. A *train* of *rolls* for reducing iron *piles* or steel ingots, blooms, or *billets* to bars of any of the various round, square, flat, or other shapes, known as merchant iron or steel.

Mercury-ores. Native mercury ; *cinnabar* (sulphide).

Merrit-plate. See *Bloomary*.

Metal, SP. 1. This term is applied both to the ore and to the metal extracted from it. It is sometimes used for vein, and even for a mine itself. *Metal en piedra*, ore in the rough state. *Metal ordinario*, common ore. *Metal pepena*, selected ore. *Metal de ayuda*, ore used to assist the smelting of other ores. 2. Copper *regulus* or *matt* obtained in the *English process*. The following varieties are distinguished by appearance and by their percentage of copper (here given in approximate figures): *Coarse*, 20 to 40; *red*, 48 ; *blue*, 60 ; *sparkle*, 74 ; *white*, 77 ; *pimple*, 79. *Fine metal* includes the latter four varieties. *Hard metal* is impure copper containing a large amount of tin. 3. SCOT. All the rocks met with in mining ore. 4. *Road metal*, rock used in macadamizing roads.

Metal-notch. See *Tap-hole*.

Mica-powder. See *Explosives*.

Mill. 1, ENG. That part of an iron works where *puddle-bars* are converted into *merchant-iron, i. e.*, rolled iron ready for sale in bars, rods, or sheets. See *Forge*. 2. By common usage, any establishment for reducing ores by other means than smelting. More strictly, a place or a machine in which ore or rock is crushed. 3. An excavation made in the *country* rock, by a *cross-cut* from the workings on a vein, to obtain waste for *gobbing*. It is left without timber so that the roof may fall in and furnish the required rock. 4. CORN. A passage through which ore is shot underground. See *Pass* and *Shoot*.

Mill-cinder. The slag from the puddling-furnaces of a rolling-mill.

Mill-run, PAC. 1. The work of an amalgamating mill between two *clean-ups.* 2. A test of a given quantity of ore by actual treatment in a mill.

Mine. 1. In general, any excavation for minerals. More strictly, subterranean workings, as distinguished from *quarries, placer* and *hydraulic* mines, and surface or open works. The distinction between the French terms *mine* and *minière* results entirely from the law, and depends upon the depth of the working. The former is the more general term, and, ordinarily speaking, includes the latter, which signifies shallow or surface workings. 2. In a military sense, a mine is a subterranean gallery run under an enemy's works, to be subsequently exploded.

Mine-pig, ENG. See *Pig-iron.*

Miner, PENN. The workman who *cuts* the coal, as distinguished from the *laborer* who loads the wagons, etc.

Mineral. In miners' parlance, ore.

Mineral caoutchouc. Elastic bitumen.

Mineral charcoal. A pulverulent, lustreless substance, showing distinct vegetable structure, and containing a high percentage of carbon with little hydrogen and oxygen, occurring in thin layers in bituminous coal.

Mineralized. Charged or impregnated with metalliferous mineral.

Mineral oil or *Naphtha.* A limpid or yellowish liquid, lighter than water, and consisting of hydrocarbons. *Petroleum* is heavier than naphtha, and dark greenish in color when crude. Both exude from the rocks; but naphtha can be distilled from petroleum.

Mineral pitch. Asphaltum.

Mineral right. The ownership of the minerals under a given surface, with the right to enter thereon, mine, and remove them. It may be separated from the surface ownership, but, if not so separated by distinct conveyance, the latter includes it.

Mineral wool. See *Slag-wool.*

Mine-rent. The rent or royalty paid to the owner of a mineral right by the operator of the mine—usually dependent, above a fixed minimum, upon the quantity of product.

Mineria, SP. Mining. This term embraces the whole subject, including both mines and miners, and also the operations of working mines and of reducing their ores. It, however, is often used in a more restricted sense.

Minero, SP. Miner. This term is not limited to those who work mines, but includes their owners, and all who have the qualifications prescribed in the ordinances, and are enrolled as members of the body or craft. Many of the laborers who work in mines are not, technically speaking, miners. This term is sometimes used in the old laws for *mine*.

Miners' inch, PAC. A local unit for the measurement of water supplied to hydraulic miners. It is the amount of water flowing under a certain head through one square inch of the total section of a certain opening, for a certain number of hours daily. All these conditions vary at different localities. At Smartsville, Cal., the discharge opening is a horizontal slit, 4 inches wide, in a 2-inch plank, with the standing head of water in the feed-box 9 inches above the middle of the slit. Each square inch of this opening will discharge 1.76 cubic feet per minute. A miners' inch in use in Eldorado County, Cal., discharges 1.39 cubic feet per minute. At North Bloomfield, Cal., and other places, the discharge is 50 inches long by 2 wide (giving 100 miners' inches) through a 3-inch plank, with the water 7 inches above the centre of the opening. Each inch is 1.50 to 1.57 cubic feet per minute in practice, or 59.05 to 61.6 per cent. of the theoretical discharge. These figures are taken from the paper of A. J. Bowie, Jr., on "Hydraulic Mining in California," *Trans. Am. Inst. M. E.*, vol. vi, p. 59.

Mineta, SP. A little mine; a chamber, or cavity.

Minium. Protosesquioxide of lead.

Mispickel, GERM. Arsenical pyrites.

Mistress, NEWC. A lantern used in coal-mines.

Mobby, S. STAFF. A leathern girdle, with small chain attached, used by the boys who draw *bowkes*.

Mock-lead, CORN. Zincblende.

Moil or *Moyle*, CORN. A drill pointed like a *gad*.

Monkey-drift. A small prospecting drift.

Monitor, PAC. A kind of nozzle used in *hydraulicking*.

Monnier process. The treatment of copper sulphide ores by roasting with sodium sulphate, and subsequent lixiviation and precipitation.

Monoclinal. Applied to any limited portion of the earth's crust throughout which the strata dip in the same direction.

Montefiore furnace. A peculiar furnace in which *zinc-dust* is compressed at a high temperature.

Moorstone, CORN. Loose masses of granite found on Cornish moors.

More, CORN. A quantity of ore in a particular part of a lode, as a *more* of tin.

Mortar. 1. A heavy iron vessel, in which rock is crushed by hand with a pestle, for sampling or assaying. 2. The receptacle beneath the stamps in a stamp mill, in which the dies are placed, and into which the rock is fed to be crushed.

Mosaic gold. Disulphide of tin.

Mote. See *Squib*.

Mothergate, NEWC. The main passage in a district of workings.

Mottled. See *Iron*.

Mouth. The end of a shaft or adit emerging at the surface.

Mountain limestone. The English designation of a limestone of the lower part of the carboniferous age; called also subcarboniferous limestone.

Muck-bar. Bar-iron which has passed once through the *rolls*.

Mucks, S. STAFF. See *Smut*.

Muffle. A semi-cylindrical or long arched oven (usually small and made of fire-clay), heated from outside, in which substances may be exposed at high temperature to an oxidizing atmospheric current, and kept at the same time from contact with the gases from the fuel. *Cupellation* and *scorification* assays are performed in *muffles*, and on a larger scale copper ores were formerly roasted in *muffle-furnaces*.

Muller. The stone or iron in an *arrastre*, or grinding or amalgamating pan, which is dragged around on the bed to grind and mix the ore-bearing rock.

Mun, CORN. Any fusible metal.

Mundic, CORN. Iron pyrites. White *mundic* is *mispickel*.

Narrow work. The driving of *gangways* or *airways*; also, any *dead work*.

Nasmyth hammer. A steam-hammer, having the head attached to the piston-rod, and operated by the direct force of the steam.

Native. Occurring in nature; not artificially formed. Usually applied to the metals.

Nays, CORN. See *Nogs*.

Needle or *Nail*, CORN. A copper or copper-pointed implement, placed in a bore-hole during charging, to make, by its withdrawal, an aperture for the insertion of the *rush* or train.

Negrillo, SP. A silver-ore; black sulphuret of silver.

Neptune powder. See *Explosives.*

Neutral. Of slags, neither acid nor basic; of wrought-irons, neither *red-short* nor *cold-short;* of iron-ores, suitable for the production of neutral irons.

Niccoliferous or *Nickeliferous.* Containing nickel.

Nickel ores. Copper-nickel (*niccolite*, arsenide of nickel); antimonial nickel (*breithauptite*, antimonide): *white nickel* (*rammelsbergite*, binarsenide); *nickel pyrites* (*pentlandite*, sulphide of nickel and iron, *millerite*, sulphide); *nickeliferous gray antimony* (*ullmannite*, arsenantimonide); *nickeliferous serpentine* (*refdanskite*, hydrous magnesian silicate); also, niccoliferous ores of copper, cobalt, manganese, etc.

Nicking, NEWC. The cutting made by the *hewer* at the side of the *face. Nickings* is the small coal produced in making the nicking.

Nicking-trunk. A tub in which metalliferous slimes are washed.

Nip, NEWC. 1. A crush of pillars or workings. 2. See *Pinch.*

Nipping-fork. A tool for supporting a column of bore-rods while raising or lowering them.

Nitroglycerin. See *Explosives.*

Nittings. The refuse of good ore.

Noble metals. The metals which have so little affinity for oxygen (*i. e.*, are so highly electronegative) that their oxides are reduced by the mere application of heat without a reagent; in other words, the metals least liable to oxidation under ordinary conditions. The list includes gold, silver, mercury, and the platinum group (including palladium, iridium, rhodium, ruthenium, and osmium). The term is of alchemistic origin.

Noddle or *Nodule.* A small rounded mass.

Noger. A *jumper* drill.

Nogs, DERB. and CORN. Square blocks or logs of wood, piled on one another to support a mine roof.

Nose. An accumulation of chilled material around the inner end of a *tuyere* in a smelting shaft-furnace, protecting and prolonging the tuyere.

Nose-helve, ENG. See *Frontal hammer.*

Nuts. Small coal.

Occlusion. The mechanical retention of gases in the pores of solids.

Ochre. A term applied to metallic oxides occurring in an earthy, pulverulent condition, as iron ochre, molybdic ochre.

Oil-well. A dug or bored well, from which petroleum is obtained by pumping or by natural flow.

Old man. Ancient workings; *goaves.*

Old men. The persons who worked a mine at any former period of which no record remains.

Open cast, SCOT. See *Open cut.*

Open-crib timbering. Shaft timbering with *cribs* alone, placed at intervals.

Open cut. A surface-working, open to daylight.

Open-front. The arrangement of a blast furnace with a *fore-hearth.*

Open-hearth. See *Reverberatory furnace.*

Openings. The parts of coal mines between the pillars, or the pillars and ribs.

Opens. Large caverns.

Open-sand castings. Castings made in moulds simply excavated in sand, without *flasks.*

Open-work. A quarry or *open cut.*

Operator, PENN. The person, whether proprietor or lessee, actually operating a colliery.

Ore. 1. A natural mineral compound, of the elements of which one at least is a metal. The term is applied more loosely to all metalliferous rock, though it contain the metals in a free state, and occasionally to the compounds of non-metallic substances, as *sulphur ore.* 2. CORN. Copper-ore; tin-ore being spoken of in Cornwall as *tin.*

Ore-hearth. See *Scotch hearth.*

Ore-washer. A machine for washing clay and earths out of earthy brown-hematite ores.

Orpiment. Sesquisulphide of arsenic.

Outbye or *Outbyeside,* NEWC. Nearer to the shaft, and hence further from the *forewinning.*

Outcrop. The portion of a vein or stratum emerging at the surface, or appearing immediately under the soil and surface-*débris.*

Outlet. The passage by which the ventilating current goes out of a mine. See *Upcast.*

Output. The product of a mine.

Oval groove. A groove of U-section in a *roll.*

Overburden. 1. CORN. See *Burden* (1). 2. To charge in a furnace too much ore and flux in proportion to the amount of fuel. 3. The waste which overlies the good stone in a quarry.

Overman, Eng. The mining official next in rank below the *manager*, who is next below the *agent*.
Overpoled copper. Copper from which all the suboxide has been removed by *poling*.
Oxidation. A chemical union with oxygen.

Pack. A wall or pillar built of *gob* to support the roof.
Pair or *Pare*, Corn. Two or more miners working in common.
Pan. 1. See *Panning*. 2. A cylindrical vat of iron, stone, or wood, or these combined, in which ore is ground with *mullers* and amalgamated. See *Amalgamation*.
Pane. The striking-face of a hammer.
Panel. 1. A heap of dressed ore. 2. A system of coal-extraction in which the ground is laid off in separate districts or panels, pillars of extra size being left between.
Panning, Aust. and Pac. Washing earth or crushed rock in a pan, by agitation with water, to obtain the particles of greatest specific gravity which it contains (chiefly practiced for gold, also for quicksilver, diamonds, and other gems).
Parachute. 1. A kind of *safety-catch* for shaft cages. 2. In rod-boring, a *cage* with a leather cover to prevent a too rapid fall of the rods in case of accident.
Parcel, Corn. A heap of dressed ore ready for sale.
Parkes process. The desilverization of lead by treatment with zinc.
Parrot coal, Scot. See *Coal*.
Parting. 1. A small joint in coal or rock, or a layer of rock in a coal seam. 2. The separation of two metals in an alloy, especially the separation of gold and silver by means of nitric or sulphuric acid.
Parting-sand. Fine dry sand, which is sifted over the partings in a *mould* to facilitate their separation when the *flask* is opened.
Pass, Corn. 1. An opening in a mine through which ore is shot from a higher to a lower level. See *Shoot*. 2. In rolling mills the passage of the bar between the *rolls*. When the bar passes "on the flat" it is called a *flatting-pass;* if "on the edge," an *edging-pass*.
Patent fuel, Eng. The fuel produced by the agglomeration of *coal-slack* into lumps.
Patera process. See *Joachimsthal process*.
Patio, Sp. The yard where the ores are cleaned and assorted;

also, the amalgamation floor, or the Spanish process itself of amalgamating silver ores on an open floor.

Pattinson process. A process in which lead containing silver is passed through a series of melting-kettles, in each of which crystals of a poorer alloy are deposited, while the fluid bath, ladled from one kettle to the next, is proportionately richer in silver. In *mechanical pattinsonation* the operation is performed in a cylindrical vessel, in which the bath is stirred mechanically, and from which, as the richer alloy crystallizes, the poorer liquid is repeatedly drained out. *Steam pattinsonation* is a variety of the *Pattinson process*, in which steam is conducted through the lead bath to assist the refining.

Pavement. The *floor* of a mine.

Pay-streak. The zone in a vein which carries the profitable or *pay* ore.

Peach, CORN. Chlorite.

Pea-coal, PENN. See *Coal*.

Percussion-table. An inclined table, agitated by a series of shocks, and operating at the same time like a *buddle*. It may be made self-discharging and continuous by substituting for the table an endless rubber cloth, slowly moving against the current of water, as in the *Frue ranner*.

Pernot furnace or *Post-Pernot furnace.* A reverberatory puddling or smelting furnace, having a circular, inclined, revolving hearth.

Pershbecker furnace. A continuously working shaft-furnace for roasting quicksilver ores, having two fire-places at opposite sides. The fuel is wood.

Pertinencia, SP. The extent of a mining location in Mexico, to which a title is acquired by denunciation.

Peter or *peter out.* To fail gradually in size, quantity, or quality.

Pewter. An alloy of tin and lead. Other metals are often added, or the lead is replaced entirely with copper, zinc, antimony, etc.

Pick. A pick-axe with one or two points. The usual miners' pick has but one.

Picker or *Poker.* A hand chisel for *dzhuing*, held in one hand and struck with a hammer.

Pick-hammer. A hammer with a point, used in cobbing.

Pickling. Cleaning sheet-iron or wire by immersion in acid.

Pig. An ingot or cast bar of metal. See *Pig-iron*.

Pig-iron. Crude cast-iron from the blast furnace. When the furnace is tapped the molten iron flows down a *runner* moulded in sand, from which it enters the *sows* or lateral runners, flowing from these again into the *pig-beds*, the separate parallel moulds of which form the *pigs*. In each bed the ingots lie against the *sow* like suckling pigs, whence the two names. See *Iron*. *Mine-pig* is pig-iron made from ores only; *cinder-pig*, from ores with admixture of some *forge* or *mill-cinder*.

Pike. See *Pick*.

Piking. See *Cobbing*.

Pile. 1. The *fagot* or bundle of flat pieces of iron prepared to be heated to welding-heat and then rolled. 2. To make up into *piles* or *fagots*. 3. *Piles* are long thick laths, etc., answering in shafts, in loose or "quick" ground, the same purpose as *spills* in levels, *piles* being driven vertically.

Pillar-and-stall. See *Post-and-stall*.

Pilz furnace. A circular or octagonal shaft-furnace, maintaining or increasing its diameter towards the top, and having several *tuyeres*; used in smelting lead-ores.

Pinch, CORN. To contract in width.

Pink ash, PENN. See *Coal*.

Pipe or **Pipe-vein,** DERB. An ore-body of elongated form.

Pipe-clay, U. S. A fine clay found in hydraulic mines.

Pipe-ore. Iron ore (limonite) in vertical pillars, sometimes of conical, sometimes of hour-glass form, imbedded in clay. Probably formed by the union of stalactites and stalagmites in caverns.

Piping. 1. PAC. See *Hydraulicking*. 2. The tubular depression caused by contraction during cooling, on the top of iron or steel ingots.

Pit. 1. A shaft. 2. A stack or *meiler* of wood, prepared for the manufacture of charcoal.

Pitch, CORN. 1. The limits of the *set* to tributers. 2. The inclination of a vein, or of the longer axis of an ore-body.

Pitch-bag, CORN. A bag covered with pitch, in which powder is inclosed for charging damp holes.

Pit-coal. See *Coal*.

Pit-eye, ENG. The bottom of the shaft of a coal-mine; also the junction of a shaft and a level.

Pit-eye pillar. A barrier of coal left around a shaft to protect it from caving.

Pit-frame. The framework carrying the pit-pulley.

Pitman. 1. CORN. A man employed to examine the lifts of pumps and the drainage. 2. NEWC. A working miner.

Pitwork, CORN. The pumps and other apparatus of the engine shaft.

Place. See *In place.*

Placer, SP. A deposit of valuable mineral, found in particles in *alluvium* or *diluvium*, or beds of streams, etc. Gold, tin ore, chromic iron, iron ore, and precious stones are found in placers. By the United States Revised Statutes all deposits not classed as veins of rock in place are considered placers.

Plane. An incline, with tracks, upon which materials are raised in cars by means of a stationary engine, or are lowered by gravity.

Plank-timbering. The lining of a shaft with rectangular plank frames.

Plank-tubbing. The lining of a shaft with planks, spiked on the inside of *curbs.*

Plat. The map of a survey in horizontal projection.

Plate-metal. See *metal.*

Plate-shale. A hard argillaceous bed.

Platinum-ores. Mixtures of native platinum in grains with various other metals and minerals.

Platt, CORN. An enlargement of a level near a shaft, where ore may await hoisting, wagons pass each other, etc.

Plattner process. See *Chlorination.*

Plomo, SP. Lead. *Plomo-plata*, lead-silver.

Plug. A hammer closely resembling the *bully.*

Plumb. 1. Vertical. 2. Soft.

Plumbago. Graphite.

Plunger. The piston of a force-pump.

Plush-copper. Chalcotrichite, a fibrous red copper ore.

Pocket. 1. A small body of ore. 2. A natural underground reservoir of water. 3. A receptacle, from which coal, ore, or waste is loaded into wagons or cars.

Podar. See *Mundic.*

Pointed boxes. Boxes in the form of inverted pyramids or wedges in which ores, after crushing and sizing, are separated in a current of water.

Pole-tools. The tools used in drilling with rods. See *Cable-tools.*

Poling. Stirring a metallic bath (of copper, tin or lead) with a pole of green wood, to cause ebullition and deoxidation in the refining process.

Polings. Poles used instead of planks for *lagging.*

Poll, CORN. The head or striking part of a miner's hammer.

Poll-pick. A pick with a head for breaking away hard *partings* in coal-seams or knocking down rock already seamed by *blasting*.

Polroz (pronounced *Polrose*), CORN. The pit underneath a water-wheel.

Ponsard furnace. A furnace in which the escaping combustion-gases, passing through tubular flues, heat the incoming air continuously through the flue-walls.

Poppet-heads, CORN. A timber frame over a shaft to carry the hoisting pulley.

Post. 1. A pillar of coal or ore. 2. An upright timber.

Post furnace. See *Pernot furnace.*

Post-and-stall. A mode of working coal, in which so much is left as pillar and so much is taken away, forming *rooms* and *thirlings.* The method is called also *bord-and-pillar, pillar-and-breast,* etc.

Potstone. Compact steatite.

Potter's clay and *Pipe-clay.* Pure plastic clay, free from iron, and consequently white after burning.

Power-drill. See *Rock-drill.*

Precious metals. See *Noble metals.*

Precipitation process. The treatment of lead ores by direct fusion with metallic iron or slags or ores rich in iron; performed generally in a *shaft-furnace,* rarely in a *reverberatory.* Often combined with the *roasting and reduction process.*

Prian, CORN. Soft white clay.

Pricker. See *Needle.*

Prill, CORN. 1. The best ore after cobbing. 2. See *Button.*

Pringap. The distance between two mining possessions in Derbyshire.

Produce. 1. The marketable ores or minerals produced by mining and *dressing.* 2. CORN. The amount of fine copper in one hundred parts of ore.

Producer. See *Gas-producer.*

Prop. A timber set to carry a roof or other weight acting by compression in the direction of the axis.

Prop-crib timbering. Shaft-timbering with *cribs* kept at the proper distance apart by means of *props.*

Prospecting. Searching for new deposits; also, preliminary explorations to test the value of lodes or placers. The *prospect* is good or bad.

Proving-hole. A small *heading* driven to find and follow a coal-seam, lost by a dislocation.

Pryan. Ore in small pebbles mixed with clay.

Pudding-stone. A conglomerate in which the pebbles are rounded. See *Breccia.*

Puddle-bars. See *Forge.*

Puddle-steel. See *Steel.*

Puddle-train. A *train* of *rolls* for reducing squeezed *puddle-balls* to *puddle* or *muck-bars.*

Puddling. 1. The process of decarburizing cast iron by fusion on the hearth of a reverberatory furnace, lined (*fixed* or *fettled*) with ore or other material rich in oxide of iron. The bath is stirred with a *rabble* to expose it to the action of the lining and of an air current. The escape of carbonic oxide causes it to boil, whence the early name of this method of puddling, viz., *boiling*. *Dry puddling* is performed on a silicious hearth, and the conversion is effected rather by the flame than by the reaction of solid or fused materials. As the amount of carbon diminishes the mass becomes less fusible and begins to coagulate (*come to nature*), after which it is worked together into lumps (*puddle balls, loups*) and removed from the furnace to be hammered (*shingled*) or *squeezed* in the *squeezer,* which presses out the *cinder,* etc., and compacts the mass at welding heat, preparatory to rolling. Silicon and phosphorus are also largely removed by puddling, passing into the cinder. Mechanical *puddlers* (in which the bath is agitated by revolution, or by mechanical *rabbles,* to save hand-labor) are employed to a limited extent. 2. The term *puddling,* now applied in metallurgy exclusively to the above process, originally referred to the *puddling* of clay or clay and charcoal upon the masonry of a furnace hearth, to form a lining. Ditches, reservoirs, etc., are *puddled* with clay to make them water-tight.

Pug-tub. See *Settler.*

Pulley-frame. Gallows-frame.

Pulp, PAC. Pulverized ore and water; also applied to dry-crushed ore.

Pulp-assay, PAC. The assay of samples taken from the *pulp* after or during crushing.

Pump-bob. See *Bob.*

Pump-rod. The rod or system of rods (usually heavy beams) connecting the steam-engine at the surface, or at a higher level, with the pump-piston below. See *Balance-bob.*

Pump-station. See *Station.*

Punch or *Puncheon.* See *Leg.*

Punch-prop, NEWC. A short *prop.*

Put, NEWC. To convey coal from the working *breast* to the tramway. This is usually done by young men (*putters*).

Putty-powder. Crude oxide of tin, used for giving opaque whiteness to enamels, or for grinding glass.

Put-work. See *Tut-work.*

Pyrometer. An instrument for measuring high temperatures.

Quarry. An open or "day" working, usually for the extraction of building-stone, slate, or limestone.

Quartation. The separation of gold from silver by dissolving out the latter with nitric acid. It requires not less than ¾ silver in the alloy, whence the name, which is also applied to the alloying of gold with silver, if necessary, to prepare it for this method of *parting.*

Quartz. 1. Crystalline silica. 2. PAC. Any hard gold or silver ore, as distinguished from gravel or earth. Hence *quartz-mining*, as distinguished from hydraulic, etc.

Quartzose. Containing quartz as a principal ingredient.

Quere, queere or *queear*, CORN. A small cavity or fissure.

Quick. 1. Applied to a productive vein as distinguished from *dead* or barren. 2. PAC. Quicksilver.

Quick ground. Ground in a loose incoherent state.

Quicksand. Sand which is (or becomes, upon the access of water) "quick," *i. e.*, shifting, easily movable or semi-liquid.

Quicksilver-ores. See *Mercury-ores.*

Quintal. One hundred pounds avoirdupois.

Rabble. An iron bar bent to a right angle at the end. See *Puddling.*

Race. A small thread of spar or ore.

Rack, CORN. A stationary *huddle.*

Rafter-timbering. Timbering in which the pieces are arranged like the rafters of a house.

Rag-burning, CORN. See *Tin-witts.*

Ragging. A rough *cobbing.*

Rail-train. A *train* of *rolls* for reducing iron *piles* or steel *ingots* or *blooms* to rails.

Raise. See *Rise.*

Rake, DERB. A fissure vein crossing the strata.

Raking-prop. An inclined *prop.*

Ramble, NEWC. A shale bed on the top of a coal seam, which falls as the coal is removed.

Rancho, SP. An estate or property; a farm (PAC. *ranch*).

Random. The direction of a *rake-vein.*

Rapper. A lever or hammer at the top of a shaft or inclined plane, for signals from the bottom.

Raschette furnace. A shaft furnace used in lead, copper, and iron smelting, and having an oblong rectangular or oval horizontal section.

Reaction process. See *Roasting and reaction process.*

Realgar. Sulphide of arsenic.

Reamer. A tool for enlarging a bore-hole.

Record. To enter in the book of the proper officer (usually a district or county officer) the name, position, description, and date of a mining claim or location. See *District.*

Red-ash, PENN. See *Coal.*

Redevance, FR. A tax, duty, or rent. In mining law it means a tax or duty payable to the government or to the surface owner.

Red-lead. See *Minium.*

Red-short. Brittle at red heat. See *Cold-short.*

Reduce. 1. To deprive of oxygen. 2. In general, to treat metallurgically for the production of metal.

Reed, CORN. See *Spire.*

Reef, AUSTR. See *Lode.*

Refinery. See *Run-out fire.*

Refining. 1. The purification of crude metallic products. The refining of "base bullion" (silver-lead) produces nearly pure lead and silver. 2. The conversion of gray into white cast iron in a *run-out fire.*

Refractory. Resisting the action of heat and chemical reagents; a quality undesirable in ores, but desirable in furnace-linings, etc.

Regenerator. A chamber, filled with open-work of brick, to take up the heat of the gases of combustion from a furnace, and subsequently impart it to a current of air, the air and gas being conducted alternately through the chamber. See *Siemens furnace.*

Regule, FR. A copper *regulus* from which most of the impurities have been removed by liquation.

Regulus. 1. The metallic mass which sinks to the bottom of a furnace or crucible, separating itself by gravity from the supernatant *slag* or *matt.* 2. An intermediate product obtained in smelting ores, specially those of copper, lead, silver and nickel, and consisting chiefly of metallic sulphides. In this sense it is synonymous with *matt*, or the GERM. *Stein*. *Antimony regulus* is metallic antimony.

Rend-rock. See *Explosives.*

Renk, NEWC. The average distance coal is brough by the *putters*.

Rests. The arrangement at the top and bottom of a pit for supporting the shaft-cage while changing the tubs or cars.

Retorting. Removing the mercury from an amalgam by volatilizing it in an iron retort, conducting it away, and condensing it.

Reverberatory furnace. A furnace in which ores are submitted to the action of flame, without contact with the fuel. The flame enters from the side or end, passes upward over a low wall or *bridge*, strikes the roof (*arch*) of the furnace, and is *reverberated* downward upon the charge.

Reversing rolls. See *Three-high train.*

Rib. 1. In coal mining, the solid coal on the side of a gallery or long-wall face; a pillar or barrier of coal left for support. 2. The solid ore of a vein; an elongated pillar left to support the hanging-wall, in working out a vein.

Ribbed. Containing *bone.*

Ribbon-borer. A boring-tool consisting of a twisted flat steel blade.

Rick, PENN. An open heap or pile in which coal is coked.

Riddle, CORN. and SCOT. A sieve. The large pieces of ore and rock picked out by hand are called *knockings*. The *riddlings* remain on the riddle; the *fell* goes through.

Rider. See *Horse.*

Riffle. A groove or interstice, or a cleat or block so placed as to produce the same effect, in the bottom of a sluice, to catch free gold.

Rim-rock. The bed-rock rising to form the boundary of a placer or gravel deposit.

Ring, NEWC. A gutter cut around a shaft to catch and conduct away the water.

Ringe. See *Cowl.*

Rise or *Riser*, CORN. A shaft or winze excavated upward.

Rise-heading. See *Heading, in long-wall.*

Rivelaine. A pick with one or two points, formed of flat iron, used to undercut coal by scraping instead of striking.

Roasting. Calcination, usually with oxidation. *Good, dead*, or *sweet roasting* is complete roasting, *i. e.*, carried on until sulphurous and arsenious fumes cease to be given off. *Kernel-roasting* is a process of treating poor sulphuretted copper ores, by roasting in lumps, whereby copper (and nickel) are concentrated in the interior of the lumps.

Roasting and reaction process. The treatment of galena in a *reverberatory*, by first partially *roasting* at a low temperature, and then partially fusing the charge at a higher temperature, which causes a reaction between the lead-oxide formed by roasting and the remaining sulphide, producing sulphurous acid and metallic lead.

Roasting and reduction process. The treatment of lead ores by roasting to form lead-oxide, and subsequent reducing fusion in a shaft-furnace.

Rob. To extract pillars previously left for support; or, in general, to take out ore or coal from a mine with a view to immediate product, and not to subsequent working.

Rock-breaker. Usually applied to a class of machines, of which Blake's rock-breaker is the type, and in which the rock is crushed between two jaws, both movable, or one fixed and one movable. It is common to use a rock-breaker instead of hand-spalling to prepare ore for further crushing in the stamp-mill.

Rock-drill. A machine for boring in rock, either by percussion, effected by reciprocating motion, or abrasion, effected by rotary motion. Compressed air is the usual motive power, but steam also is used. The Burleigh, Haupt, Ingersoll, Wood, and other machines operate percussively; the *diamond drill* (which see) abrasively.

Rocker. A short trough in which auriferous sands are agitated by oscillation, in water, to collect their gold.

Rod-tools. See *Pole-tools.*

Rolley. A large truck carrying two *corves.*

Rolley-way. A *gangway.*

Rolling. See *Roll-train.*

Rolls. 1. Cylinders of iron or steel revolving towards each other, between which rock is made to pass, in order to crush it. 2. See *Roll-train.*

Roll-train. The set of plain or grooved rolls through which iron or steel *piles, ingots, blooms,* or *billets* are passed, to be rolled into various shapes.

Rondle or *Rondelle.* The crust or scale which forms upon the surface of molten metal in cooling.

Roof. The rock overlying a bed or flat vein.

Roofing. The wedging of a loaded wagon or horse against the top of an underground passage.

Room, Scot. See *Breast* and *Post-and-stall.*

Rosette copper. Disks of copper (red from the presence of suboxide) formed by cooling the surface of molten copper through sprinkling with water.

Rossie furnace. An American variety of hearth for the treatment of galena, differing from the *Scotch hearth* in using wood as fuel, working continuously, and having hollow walls, to heat the blast.

Roughing rolls. The *rolls* of a *train* which first receive the *pile*, *ingot*, *bloom*, or *billet*, and partially form it into the final shape.

Roughs, CORN. Coarse, poor sands, resulting from tin-dressing.

Round coal. See *Lump-coal.*

Rounder. See *Reamer.*

Row, CORN. Large, rough stones.

Royalty. The dues of the lessor or landlord of a mine, or of the owner of a patented invention.

Rozan process. An improvement of the *Pattinson process.*

Rubber. A gold-quartz amalgamator, in which the slime is rubbed against amalgamated copper surfaces.

Rullers, CORN. The workmen who wheel ore in wheelbarrows underground.

Run, CORN. 1. The natural falling or closing together of underground workings. 2. Certain accidents to the winding apparatus. 3. *By the run.* A method of paying coal miners per linear yard of breast excavated, instead of *by the wagon* of clear coal produced. 4. A long deep-trough in which slimes settle. 5. See *Counter.*

Runner. The channel through which molten metal is conducted from the blast furnace or cupola to the *pig-bed*, *converter* or *moulds.* See *Pig-iron.*

Run-out fire. A forge in which cast-iron is refined.

Run-steel. Malleable castings.

Rush, CORN. See *Spire.*

Rusty. Applied to coals discolored by water or exposure, as well as to quartz, etc., discolored by iron oxide.

Rusty gold, PAC. Free gold, which does not easily amalgamate, the particles being coated, as is supposed, with oxide of iron.

Saddle. An anticlinal in a bed or flat vein.

Safety-cage. A cage with a *safety catch.*

Safety-car. See *Barney.*

Safety-catch. An automatic device for preventing the fall of a cage in a shaft or a car in an incline, if the supporting cable breaks

Safety-lamp. A lamp, the flame of which is so protected that it will not immediately ignite fire-damp. There are several varieties, invented by Davy, Stephenson, Clanny, and others.

Salamander. A mass of solidified material in a furnace hearth; called also a *sow* and *bear*.

Saline. A salt spring or well; salt works.

Sampson-post. An upright post which supports the walking-beam, communicating motion from the engine to a deep-boring apparatus.

Sand-pump. A cylinder with a valve at the bottom, lowered into a drill-hole from time to time, to take out the accumulated slime resulting from the action of the drill on the rock. Called, also, *Shell-pump* and *Sludger*.

Scaffold. An obstruction in a *blast furnace* above the *tuyeres* caused by an accumulation or shelf of pasty, unreduced materials, adhering to the lining.

Seal, CORN. A portion of earth or rock which separates and falls from the main body.

Scale. 1. The crust of metallic oxide formed by cooling of hot metals in air. *Hammer-scale* and *roll-scale* are the flaky oxides which fall from the *bloom, ingot*, or *bar* under hammering or rolling. 2. The incrustation caused in steam-boilers by the evaporation of water containing mineral salts. 3. A *scale of air* (NEWC.) is a small portion of air abstracted from the main current.

Scarcement. A projecting ledge of rock, left in a shaft as footing for a ladder, or to support pit-work, etc.

Scarfing. Splicing timbers, so cut that when joined the resulting piece is not thicker at the joint than elsewhere.

Schist. Crystalline rock, usually micaceous, having a slaty structure.

Schlicker, GERM. The skimmings from molten unrefined lead, containing chiefly copper, iron, and zinc, with a little antimony and arsenic.

Schorl. Black tourmaline.

Scoria or *Scoriæ*. See *Slag*.

Scorification. A process employed in assaying gold and silver ores, and performed in a shallow clay vessel (*scorifier*), in which ore, lead, and borax-glass are exposed to heat and oxidation in a *muffle*. The operation involves roasting, fusion, and *scorification* proper, or the formation of a slag, which is not, like the litharge produced in *cupellation*, absorbed by the vessel.

Scotch hearth. A low forge or furnace of cast-iron, with one *tuyere*, in which rich galena is treated by a sort of accelerated *roasting and reaction process.*

Scouring cinder. A basic slag, which attacks the lining of a shaft-furnace.

Scoran lode, CORN. A lode having no *gossan* at or near the surface.

Scraper. A tool for cleaning bore-holes.

Screen. A sieve of wire-cloth, grate-bars, or perforated sheet-iron used to sort ore and coal according to size. Stamp-mortars have screens on one or both sides, to determine the fineness of the escaping pulp.

Screw-bell. A recovering tool in deep boring, ending below in a hollow screw-threaded cone.

Scrin or *Skrin,* DERB. A small subordinate vein.

Seam. 1. A stratum or bed of coal or other mineral. 2. CORN. A horse-load. 3. A *joint, cleft,* or *fissure.*

Seat, DERB. The floor of a mine.

Seed-bag. A bag filled with flaxseed and fastened around the tubing in an artesian well, so as to form, by the swelling of the flaxseed when wet, a water-tight packing, preventing percolation down the sides of the bore-hole from upper to lower strata. When the tubing is pulled up the upper fastening of the bag breaks, and it empties itself, thus presenting no resistance to the extraction of the tubing.

Segregate, PAC. To separate the undivided joint ownership of a mining claim into smaller individual "*segregated*" claims.

Segregation. A mineral deposit formed by concentration from the adjacent rock.

Selvage, or *Selfedge.* A layer of clay or decomposed rock along a vein-wall. See *Gouge.*

Semi-anthracite. See *Coal.*

Semi-bituminous coal. See *Coal.*

Separator. 1. A machine for separating, with the aid of water or air, materials of different specific gravity. Strictly, a *separator* parts two or more ingredients, both valuable, while a *concentrator* saves but one and rejects the rest; but the terms are often used interchangeably. 2. Any machine for separating materials, as the *magnetic separator,* for separating magnetite from its gangue.

Set or *Sett,* CORN. 1. A grant of mining ground, as the assignment of a certain part of a mine under contract or *tribute.* 2. A frame of timber for supporting excavations.

Settler. A tub or vat, in which *pulp* from the amalgamating *pan* or *battery-pulp* is allowed to settle, being stirred in water, to remove the lighter portions.

Shadd, CORN. Smooth, round stones on the surface, containing tin-ore, and indicating a vein.

Shaft. 1. A pit sunk from the surface. 2. The interior of a *shaft-furnace* above the boshes.

Shaft-furnace. A high furnace, charged at the top and tapped at the bottom.

Shaft-walls. 1. The sides of a shaft. 2. NEWC. Pillars of coal left near the bottom of a pit.

Shake. 1. A cavern, usually in limestone. 2. A crack in a block of stone.

Shaking-table. See *Percussion-table.*

Shambles. Shelves or benches, from one to the other of which successively ore is thrown in raising it to the level above, or to the surface.

Shearing. 1. The vertical side-cutting which, together with *holing* or horizontal undercutting, constitutes the attack upon a *face* of coal. 2. Cutting up steel for the crucible.

Shears, CORN. Two high timbers, standing over a shaft and united at the top to carry a pulley, for lifting or lowering timbers, pipes, etc., of greater length than the ordinary hoisting-gear can accommodate.

Sheathing. A close partition or covering of planks.

Sheave. The groove-wheel of a pulley.

Shelf, CORN. The solid rock or *bed-rock,* especially under alluvial tin-deposits.

Shell-pump. See *Sand-pump.*

Shelly. The condition of coal which has been so much faulted and twisted that it is not massive, but easily breaks into conchoidal pieces.

Shet, S. STAFF. The broken-down roof of a coal-mine.

Shift. 1. The time for a miner's work in one day. 2. The gang of men working for that period, as the *day-shift,* the *night-shift.*

Shift-boss. The foreman in charge of a *shift* of men.

Shingling. Hammering *blooms, billets,* etc.

Shiver. 1. Shale; a hard argillaceous bed. 2. See *Sheave.*

Shoad, CORN. Ore washed or detached from the vein naturally. See *Float-ore.*

Shoading or *Shoding*, Corn. The tracking of boulders towards the vein or rock from which they have come.

Shoe. A piece of iron or steel, attached to the bottom of a *stamp* or *muller*, for grinding ore. The shoe can be replaced when worn out.

Shoot. 1. See *Chute*. 2. See *Blast*. A *shot* is a single operation of *blasting*.

Shooting-needle. A sharp metal rod, to form a vent-hole through the tamping to a blasting-charge.

Shore-nose shell. A cylindrical tool, cut obliquely at bottom, for boring through hard clay.

Show. 1. The pale-blue, lambent flame on the top of a common candle-flame, indicating the presence of fire-damp. 2. See *Blossom*.

Shute. See *Chute*.

Sicker. See *Zighyr*.

Siddle. The inclination of a seam of coal.

Side-basset. A transverse direction to the line of dip in strata.

Side-guide. See *Guard*.

Side-laning, S. Staff. Widening a *gate-road* (abandoned for that purpose) so as to make it part of a new *side of work*.

Side of work, S. Staff. The series of *breasts* and *pillars* connected with a *gate-road* in a colliery.

Siemens furnace. A reverberatory furnace, heated by gas, with the aid of regenerators.

Sigger. See *Zighyr*.

Silesian zinc furnace. A furnace in which zinc is reduced and distilled from calcined ores in muffles.

Silicious. Consisting of or containing silex or quartz.

Sill. 1. A stratum. 2. A piece of wood laid across a drift to constitute a frame with the posts and to carry the track of the tramway.

Silt. See *Alluvium*.

Silver ores. *Silver-glance* (*argentite*, sulphide); *horn-silver* (*cerargyrite*, chloride); *dark-ruby silver* (*pyrargyrite*, sulphantimonide); *light-ruby silver* (*proustite*, sulpharsenide); *brittle silver-glance* (*stephanite*, antimonial sulphide of silver, and *polybasite*, arsenical and antimonial sulphide of several metals); *white ore* (argentiferous gray copper, *tetrahedrite*, antimonial sulphide of iron, zinc, copper, lead, and silver); *stetefeldtite* and *partzite* (antimoniates); also, argentiferous lead, copper, and zinc ores.

Sinker-bar. A heavy bar attached above the *jars* to *cable-drilling tools*.

Sinking-fire. A forge in which wrought-iron scrap or refined pig-iron is partially melted or welded together by means of a charcoal-fire and a blast.

Siphon-tap. See *Arends' tap.*

Sit or *Sits.* A settling or falling of the top of workings. See *Thrust* and *Creep.*

Sizing. Separating ores according to size of particles, preparatory to *dressing.*

Skep or *Skip*, CORN. An iron box working between guides, in which ore or rock is hoisted. It is distinguished from a *kibble*, which hangs free in the shaft.

Skew-plate. See *Bloomary.*

Skimmings or *Skimpings*, CORN. The poorest part skimmed off the *jigger.*

Skull. A crust of solidified steel lining a Bessemer ladle.

Slack. Small coal; coal dirt. See *Culm* (2).

Slag. The vitreous mass separated from the fused metals in smelting ores.

Slag-hearth. A hearth on the principle of the *Scotch-hearth* for the treatment of slags, etc., produced by lead-smelting in the reverberatory furnace. The English slag-hearth has one *tuyere*; the Castilian or Spanish, three.

Slag-lead. Lead obtained by a re-smelting of *gray slag.*

Slag-wool. A finely fibrous mass produced by blowing steam or air into molten slag.

Slant. A heading driven diagonally between the dip and the strike of a coal-seam; also called a *run.* See *Run* and *Counter.*

Slate. A sedimentary rock splitting into thin plates. The terms *slate*, *shale*, and *schist* are not sharply distinguished in common use, particularly among older writers. Strictly, according to recent authors, *slate* may be crystalline; *schist* is always so; shale is always (and *slate* most frequently) non-crystalline. There is also a notion of coarser or less complete lamination attached to the term *shale*, as of a rock splitting into thicker or less perfect plates than *slate*. Both may be argillaceous, arenaceous, calcareous, silicious, etc., according to their lithological character. The terms *slaty*, *shaly*, and *schistose* describe the respective structures.

Sleck, NEWC. Mud deposited by water in a mine.

Sleeper. See *Sill.*

Sleeping-table, CORN. A stationary *buddle.* For the strict distinction sometimes made between *buddle* and *table*, see *Buddle.*

Slickensides. Polished and sometimes striated surfaces on the walls of a vein, or on interior joints of the vein-material or of rock-masses. They are the result of movement.

Slide, CORN. 1. A vein of clay intersecting and dislocating a vein vertically; or the vertical dislocation itself. 2. An upright rail fixed in a shaft with corresponding grooves for steadying the cages.

Slide-joint. A connection acting in *rod-boring,* like the *jars* in *rope-boring.*

Slimes, CORN. The most finely crushed ores.

Slime-table. See *Buddle.*

Sline. Natural transverse cleavage of rock.

Slip. A vertical dislocation of the rocks.

Slipes, S. STAFF. Sledge-runners, upon which a *skip* is dragged from the working breast to the tramway.

Slit. A communication between two levels.

Slitter. See *Pick.*

Sliver, ENG. A thin wooden strip, inserted into grooves in the adjacent edges of two boards of a *brattice,* to make it air-tight.

Slope. See *Incline.*

Sludge. See *Slimes.*

Sludger. See *Sand-pump.*

Sluicing. Washing auriferous earth through long boxes (*sluices*).

Slums, PAC. See *Slimes.*

Slurry, N. WALES. See *Regulus* (2).

Smalt. A blue pigment or glass, consisting of silica, potash, and cobalt.

Smeddum, SCOT. The smaller particles which pass through the sieve of the *hutch.*

Smelting. Reducing ores by fusion in furnaces.

Smift. A fuse or slow match.

Smitham or *Smiddan,* DERB. Lead-ore dust.

Smut. 1. S. STAFF. Bad, soft coal, containing much earthy matter. 2. See *Blossom.*

Snoff, CORN. A short candle-end, put under a fuse to light it.

Snore-hole. The hole in the lower part or *wind-bore* of a mining pump, to admit the water.

Soapstone. Compact talc or steatite; often applied incorrectly to soft unctuous clays or marls.

Softening. Of lead, the removal of antimony and other impurities.

Solder. A metal or alloy used to unite adjacent surfaces of less fusible metals or alloys. *Soft solder* is a compound of tin and lead;

hard solder, of copper and zinc, or tin, copper, and zinc, or tin and antimony; *gold solder*, of gold, silver, and copper; *silver solder*, of silver and copper, or silver and brass; and so on.

Sole. 1. The bottom of a level. 2. The bottom of a reverberatory furnace.

Solid crib-timbering. Shaft-timbering with cribs laid solidly upon one another.

Sollar, CORN. A platform in a shaft, usually constituting a landing between two ladders.

Sough, DERB. See *Adit*.

Sow. 1. See *Salamander*. 2. See *Pig-iron*.

Spale, CORN. To fine for disobedience of orders.

Spall or *Spawl*. To break ore. *Ragging* and *cobbing* are respectively coarser and finer breaking than *spalling*, but the terms are often used interchangeably. Pieces of ore thus broken are called *spalls*.

Spar. A name given by miners to any earthy mineral having a distinct cleavable structure and some lustre; in Cornwall usually quartz.

Spears. See *Pump-rods*.

Speise or *Speiss*, GERM. Impure metallic arsenides (principally of iron), produced in copper and lead smelting. Cobalt and nickel are found concentrated in the speiss obtained from ores containing these metals

Spel or *Spell*. A change or turn.

Spence-furnace. A long *reverberatory*, for thorough roasting.

Spend. To break ground; to continue working.

Spiegeleisen. Manganiferous white cast-iron.

Spiking-curb, ENG. A curb to the inside of which *plank-tubing* is spiked.

Spilling, CORN. A process of driving or sinking through very loose ground.

Spills, CORN. Long thick laths or poles driven ahead horizontally around the door-frames, in running levels in loose ground—a kind of *lagging* put in ahead of the main timbering.

Spire. The tube carrying the train to the charge in a blast-hole. Also called *reed* or *rush*, because these, as well as spires of grass, are used for the purpose.

Spitting. The violent ejection of globules by a body of molten silver, in the act of becoming solidified by cooling.

Splint coal. See *Coal*.

Split. 1. To divide a ventilating current. 2. When a *parting* in a coal-seam becomes so thick that the two portions of the seam must be worked separately, each is called a *split.* See *Bench.*

Sponge. Metal in a porous form, usually obtained by reduction without fusion. See *Chenot process.*

Spoon. 1. An instrument made of an ox or buffalo horn, in which earth or *pulp* may be delicately tested by washing to detect gold, amalgam, etc. 2 (or *Spoon-end*). The edge of a coal-basin when the coal-seam *spoons, i. e.*, rises to the surface, after growing thinner as it approaches its termination.

Spout, S. STAFF. See *Air-head.*

Sprag. 1. A *prop.* 2. A short round piece of wood used to block the wheels of a car.

Spreader. A horizontal timber below the *cap* of a set, to stiffen the *legs,* and to support the *brattice* when there are two air-courses in the same gangway.

Spreaders. Pieces of timber stretched across a shaft as a temporary support of the walls.

Sprue. A piece of metal attached to a casting, occupying the *gate* or passage through which the metal was poured.

Spud. A nail, resembling a horseshoe nail, with a hole in the head, driven into mine-timbering, or into a wooden plug inserted in the rock, to mark a surveying-station.

Spur. A branch leaving a vein, but not returning to it.

Spurns, S. STAFF. Small connecting masses of coal, left for safety during the operation of cutting, between the *hanging coal* and the main body.

Square sets. A kind of timbering used in large spaces.

Squat, CORN. 1. Tin-ore mixed with spar. 2. See *Bunch of ore.*

Squeeze. The settling, without breaking, of the *roof* over a considerable area of workings.

Squeezer. A machine for reducing the *puddle-ball* to a compact mass, ready for the hammer or rolls.

Squib. A slow-match or safety-fuse, used with a *barrel.*

Squirting. Forcing lead by hydraulic pressure into the form of rods or pipes.

Stack. 1. A chimney. 2. See *Shaft-furnace.*

Stall, S. STAFF. See *Room, Breast,* and *Post-and-Stall.*

Stamping. Reducing to the desired fineness in a *stamp-mill.* The grain is usually not so fine as that produced by grinding in *pans.*

Stamp-mill. An apparatus (also the building containing the apparatus) in which rock is crushed by descending pestles (*stamps*), operated by water or steam-power. Amalgamation is usually combined with the crushing when gold or silver is the metal sought, but copper and tin-ores, etc., are stamped to prepare them for *dressing.*

Stamps, S. WALES. The pieces into which the rough bars *shingled* from the finery ball are broken, to be *piled* for subsequent rolling into sheet-iron.

Stamp-work, LAKE SUP. Rock containing disseminated native copper.

Stanchion. See *Leg.*

Standage, ENG. A large *sump,* or more than one, acting as a reservoir.

Stannary. A tin-mine or tin-works.

Station. 1. See *Platt.* 2. Also, a similar enlargement of shaft or level to receive a balance-bob (*bob-station*), pump (*pump-station*), or tank (*tank-station*).

Steamboat-coal, PENN. See *Coal.*

Steam-coal. See *Coal.*

Steel. A compound or alloy of iron, principally with carbon, which may be cast, forged, hardened, and tempered. Ordinary steel contains from 0.5 to 1.5 per cent. of carbon. More carbon makes cast-iron; less carbon, wrought-iron. But this classification is not now strictly adequate or applicable, either to the scientific or to the commercial use of the term. The so-called *mild* or *low* or *structural* steels (low in carbon, and hence relatively soft and tough), as compared with *high* or *hard* or *tool* steels, do not always harden or temper. An international committee appointed by the American Institute of Mining Engineers has recommended the use of the following classification:

1. That all malleable compounds of iron with its ordinary ingredients, which are aggregated from pasty masses, or from piles, or from any forms of iron not in a fluid state, and which will not sensibly harden and temper, and which generally resemble what is called "wrought-iron," shall be called *weld-iron* (GERM., *Schweisseisen;* FR., *fer soudé*).

2. That such compounds, when they will from any cause harden and temper, and which resemble what is now called "puddled steel," shall be called *weld-steel* (GERM., *Schweissstahl;* FR., *acier soudé*).

3. That all compounds of iron with its ordinary ingredients, which have been cast from a fluid state into malleable masses, and which

will not sensibly harden by being quenched in water while at a red heat, shall be called *ingot-iron* (GERM., *Flusseisen;* FR., *fer fondu*).

4. That all such compounds, when they will from any cause so harden, shall be called *ingot-steel* (GERM., *Flussstahl;* FR., *acier fondu*). This proposed classification does not cover ordinary cast or pig iron. It is a classification of the malleable compounds only. The Institute has recommended its use in papers and discussions, except as to the term *weld*, for which a substitute was desired, and meanwhile the continuance of the old term *wrought*, though in a somewhat wider significance, was suggested. The resolution of the Institute concludes as follows: " It being understood that the *ingot-iron* and *ingot-steel* of this classification constitute, taken together, what is now commercially known as *cast-steel*, including the so-called low or soft caststeels." *Bessemer-steel* is made by decarburizing cast iron in a *converter*. (See *Bessemer process*.) *Blister* or *cement-steel* is made by carburizing wrought iron bars by packing them in charcoal powder and heating without access of air. It is melted in crucibles to *cast-steel*, or hammered (*tilted*) to *shear-steel* (for cutlery, etc.), or rolled to *springsteel*. *Puddled steel* is made by arresting the *puddling* process before wrought iron has been produced, and thus retaining enough carbon in the bath to constitute steel. *Natural* steel is a similar product, obtained from the refining of cast-iron. *Crucible cast-steel* is steel made by the fusion in crucibles, either of *blister-steel*, or *puddled steel*, or steel-scrap, or other ingredients and fluxes which will produce the desired quality. *Cast-steel* in its widest sense, as now employed, comprises all malleable compounds of iron produced by fusion, including therefore the *Bessemer* and *open-hearth* metal. *Open-hearth*, called also *Martin-Siemens steel*, is made in the reverberatory furnace (almost invariably a gas-furnace on the Siemens regenerative system, since an intense temperature is required) by the reaction, in the fused bath, of cast-iron with wrought-iron, iron-oxide, or iron ore. At a certain stage of the process a *deoxidizing* or *recarburizing* agent (*spiegeleisen*, *ferromanganese*) is added. *Chrome-steel* is a crucible cast-steel in which chromium is a constituent. *Tungsten* or *Wolfram-steel* is a steel containing tungsten. *Phosphorus-steel* is a steel in which the amount of phosphorus exceeds that of carbon. *Damascus-steel* is a laminated mixture of steel and wrought iron. *India-steel* or *Wootz* is manufactured in India direct from the ore.

Stemmer, NEWC. See *Tamping-bar*.

Stemming, NEWC. The tamping put above the charge in a borehole.

Stempel or *Stemple*. 1. DERB. One of the cross-bars of wood placed in a mine-shaft to serve as steps. 2. A *stull-piece*. 3. A *cap*, both sides of which are *hitched* instead of being supported upon legs. See *Stull*.

Stenton, NBWC. A passage between two *winning headways*. A *stenton-wall* is the *pillar* of coal between them.

Step-grate. A grate made in steps or stairs, to promote completeness of the combustion of the coal burned upon it.

Step-vein. A vein alternately cutting through the strata of *country-rock*, and running parallel with them.

Stetefeldt furnace. A shaft-furnace for desulphurizing or chloridizing-roasting, in which the pulverized charge falls freely down the shaft.

Stirrup. See *Temper-screw*.

Stockwork (GERM., *Stockwerk*). An ore-deposit of such a form that it is worked in floors or stories. It may be a solid mass of ore, or a rock-mass so interpenetrated by small veins of ore that the whole must be mined together. *Stockworks* are distinguished from *tabular* or *sheet*-deposits (veins, beds), which have a small thickness in comparison with their extension in the main plane of the deposit (that is, in *strike* and *dip*).

Stone-coal. See *Coal*.

Stone-head, ENG. The solid rock first encountered in sinking a shaft.

Stoop-and-Rooms, SCOT. See *Post-and-Stall*.

Stope, CORN. To excavate ore in a vein by driving horizontally upon it a series of workings, one immediately over the other, or *vice versa*. Each horizontal working is called a stope (probably a corruption of *step*), because when a number of them are in progress, each working face being a little in advance of the next above or below, the whole face under attack assumes the shape of a flight of stairs. When the first stope is begun at a lower corner of the body of ore to be removed, and, after it has advanced a convenient distance, the next is commenced above it, and so on, the process is called *over-hand* stoping. When the first stope begins at an upper corner, and the succeeding ones are below it, it is *under-hand* stoping. The term *stoping* is loosely applied to any subterranean extraction of ore except that which is incidentally performed in sinking shafts, driving levels, etc., for the purpose of opening the mine.

Stopping. 1. See *Stoping*. 2. A partition of boards, masonry,

A GLOSSARY OF MINING AND METALLURGICAL TERMS. 85

or rubbish, to stop the air-current in a mine, or force it to take a special desired direction.

Stove. The oven in which the blast of a furnace is heated.

Stove-coal, PENN. See *Coal*.

Stowbord, NEWC. A place into which rubbish is put.

Stowce. 1. A windlass. 2. DERB. *Stowces* are wooden landmarks, placed to indicate possession of mining ground.

Stowing. A method of mining in which all the material of the vein is removed and the waste is packed into the space left by the working.

Straightening press. A power-press to straighten iron and steel bars, such as rails, shafting, etc.

Strake, CORN. An inclined *launder* for separating or *tying* ground ore in water.

Stratum. A bed or layer.

Streak. The powder of a mineral, or the mark which it makes when rubbed upon a harder surface.

Stream-tin, CORN. Tin-ore in alluvial deposits, as pebbles.

Stream-work, CORN. Work on *stream-tin*.

Streamers, CORN. Searchers for *stream-tin*.

Striated. Marked with parallel grooves or *striæ*.

Strike. The direction of a horizontal line, drawn in the middle plane of a vein or stratum not horizontal.

String, CORN. A small vein.

Stringing-deals, ENG. Thin planks, nailed to the inside of the curbs in a shaft, so as to suspend each curb from those above it.

Strip. To remove from a quarry, or other open working, the overlying earth and disintegrated or barren surface rock.

Studdles, CORN. 1. Props supporting the middle of *stulls*. 2. Distance-pieces between successive frames of timbering.

Stull, CORN. A platform (*stull-covering*), laid on timbers (*stull-pieces*), braced across a working from side to side, to support workmen or to carry ore or waste.

Stulm. See *Adit*. From the GERM. *Stollen*.

Stump, PENN. A small pillar of coal, left at the foot of a *breast* to protect the *gangway*.

Stup. A pulverized mixture of clay and coke or coal. Probably from the GERM. *Gestübbe*.

Sturt. A *tribute*-bargain which turns out profitable for the miner.

Stythe, NEWC. *Choke-damp*.

Sublimation. The volatilization and condensation of a solid substance, without fusion.

Sublimation-theory. The theory that a vein was filled first with metallic vapors.

Sucker-rod. The *pump-rod* of an oil-well.

Sulphur. 1. Iron pyrites. 2. Carburetted or sulphuretted hydrogen.

Sulphurets, PAC. In miners' phrase, the undecomposed metallic ores, usually sulphides. Chiefly applied to auriferous pyrites.

Sump, CORN. (from GERM. *Sumpf.*). The space left below the lowest landing in a shaft to collect the mine-water. The lowest pump draws from it. 2. NEWC. That part of a *judd* of coal which is extracted first.

Sump-fuse. A waterproof fuse.

Swad, NEWC. A thin layer of stone or refuse coal at the bottom of the seam.

Swape. An implement for shaping the edge of a boring-bit.

Swalls, Swallows or *Swallow-holes.* Surface holes caused by the subsidence of rocks; or openings into which mine-water disappears.

Swamp. A depression in a nearly horizontal bed, in which water may collect.

Swedish process. See *German process*.

Sweeping table. A stationary *buddle*.

Sweeps. The dust of the workshops of jewellers, goldsmiths, silversmiths, and assayers and refiners of gold and silver.

Sweet-roasting. See *Roasting*.

Synclinal. The axis of a depression of the strata; also the depression itself. Opposed to *anticlinal*, which is the axis of an elevation.

Tackle, CORN. The *windlass*, rope, and *kibble*.

Tacklers, DERB. Small chains put around loaded *corves*.

Tail-house, Tail-mill. The buildings in which *tailings* are treated.

Tailing. See *Blossom*.

Tailings. The lighter and sandy portions of the ore on a buddle or in a sluice. The *headings* are accumulated or discharged at the upper end, the *middlings* in the middle, while the *tailings* escape at the foot. The term *tailings* is used in a general sense for the refuse of reduction-processes other than smelting.

Tail-race. The channel in which *tailings*, suspended in water, are conducted away.

Tamp. To fill (usually with clay-tamping) the bore-hole or other opening through which an explosive charge has been introduced for blasting.

Tamping-bar, CORN.

Tank. A subterranean reservoir into which a pump delivers water for another pump to raise.

Tap-cinder. The cinder drawn from a *puddling*-furnace or *bloomary.*

Tap-hole. The opening through which the molten metal is *tapped* or drawn from a furnace.

Teem, ENG. 1. To dump. 2. To pour steel from a melting-pot.

Temper. 1. To grind and mix plastic materials, such as clay, or the ingredients of mortar. 2. To give the metals (especially steel) the desired degree of hardness and elasticity by a process of heating and cooling, suitably regulated. A metallic compound in which these qualities can thus be produced is said *to temper,* or *to take temper.*

Tempering-bar. See *Furgen.*

Temper-screw. A screw-connection for lengthening the column of boring-rods as boring advances.

Tenant-helve, ENG. See *Frontal-hammer.*

Tepetate, SP. Waste rock and rubbish in a mine.

Terne-plate. A variety of tin-plate coated with an alloy of one-third tin, and two-thirds lead.

Test. See *Cupel.*

Test-ring. An oval iron frame for holding a test or movable cupelling-hearth.

Thermo-aqueous. Produced by, or related to, the action of heated waters.

Thill, NEWC. The floor of a coal mine.

Thirling. See *Thurling.*

Thomas and Gilchrist process. See *Basic lining process.*

Three-high train. A *roll-train* composed of three rolls, the bar being entered on one side between the bottom and the middle roll, and on the other side between the middle and the upper roll. The *passes* in both directions thus take place without reversing the movement of the rolls, as is done in so-called *reversing rolls.*

Throw. A dislocation or fault of a vein or stratum, which has been *thrown up* or *down* by the movement.

Throwing, S. STAFF. The operation of breaking out the *spurns,* so as to leave the *hanging coal* unsupported, except by its own cohesion.

Thrust. The breaking down or the slow descent of the roof of a gangway. Compare *Creep.*

Thurl, S. STAFF. To cut through from one working into another.

Thurlings. Passages cut from room to room, in *post-and-stall* working.

Thurst. The ruins of the fallen roof, after *pillars* and *stalls* have been removed.

Ticketings, CORN. Meetings for the sale of ores.

Tick-hole. See *Tug.*

Tierras, SP. Fine dirt impregnated with quicksilver ore, which must be made into *adobes* before roasting.

Tiger. See *Nipping-fork.*

Tile-copper. See *Bottoms* (2).

Tiller. See *Brace-head.*

Tilt-hammer. A hammer for shingling or forging iron, arranged as a lever of the first or third order, and "tilted" or "tripped" by means of a cam or cog-gearing, and allowed to fall upon the billet, bloom, or bar.

Tin-frame, CORN. A *sleeping-table* used in dressing tin-ore *slimes,* and discharged by turning it upon an axis till its surface is nearly vertical, and then dashing water over it, to remove the enriched deposit. A *machine-frame* or *self-acting frame* thus discharges itself automatically at intervals; a *hand-frame* is turned for the purpose by hand.

Tin-ores. Tinstone (*cassiterite,* oxide); *tin-pyrites* (*stannite,* sulphide of tin, copper, iron and zinc). The latter is not, so far as I am aware, now actually treated for tin. Ores containing it are smelted as copper-ores, and the tin is lost.

Tin-plate. Sheet-iron coated with tin.

Tin-witts, CORN. The product of the first dressing of tin-ores, containing, besides tinstone, other heavy minerals (wolfram and metallic sulphides). It must be roasted before it can be further concentrated. Its first or partial roasting is called *rag-burning.*

Tipe. To upset or "dump" a *skip.*

Toadstone. A kind of trap-rock.

Ton. For many things, such as coal and iron, the ton in use is the *long* ton of 20 hundredweight at 112 pounds avoirdupois. Allowances ("sandage," etc.), are made in weighing pig-iron and other crude metals, so that the "smelter's ton" is still greater. The Cornish mining ton is 21 hundredweight or 2352 pounds avoirdupois.

In gold and silver mining, and throughout the Western States, the ton is the *short* ton of 2000 pounds.

Tonite. A nitrated gun-cotton, used in blasting.

Top-wall. See *Hanging-wall.*

Torta, SP. A flat heap of silver ore (*slime* or *pulp*) prepared for the *patio* process.

Tossing or *tozing,* CORN. 1. Washing ores by violent agitation in water, their subsidence being accelerated by *packing* or striking with a hammer the *keeve* in which the operation is performed. *Chimming* is a similar process on a smaller scale. 2. Refining tin by allowing it, while molten, to fall several feet through the air.

Touchstone. A black, hard stone (basalt or jasper), on which the fineness of an alloy of gold and silver can be tested by comparing its *streak* with that of a piece of alloy (*touch-needle*) of known fineness.

Tough-cake. Refined or commercial copper.

Toughening. Refining, as of copper or gold.

Tough-pitch. See *Tough-cake.*

Towl, NEWC. A piece of old rope.

Train. See *Roll-train.*

Tram, WALES. 1. A four-wheeled truck to carry a *tub, corve,* or *hutch,* or to carry coal or ore on a railroad. 2. One of the rails of a *tramroad* or railroad.

Trap. In miners' parlance, any dark, igneous or apparently igneous, or volcanic rock.

Trap-door. See *Weather-door.*

Trapiche, SP. A rude grinding machine, composed of two stones, of which the upper is fastened to a long pole.

Trapper. NEWC. A boy who opens and shuts the *trap-door.*

Tribute, CORN. A portion of ore given to the miner for his labor. *Tributors* are miners working under contract, to be paid by a *tribute* of ore or its equivalent price, the basis of the remuneration being the amount of clean ore contained in the crude product.

Trip-hammer. See *Tilt-hammer.*

Trogue. A wooden trough, forming a drain.

Trolly. A small four or two-wheeled truck, without a body. The two-wheeled trolly is used in a *rolling-mill* to wheel the *puddle-balls* to the *squeezer.*

Trombe or *Trompe,* FR. An apparatus for producing an air-blast by means of a falling stream of water, which mechanically carries air down with it, to be subsequently separated and compressed in a reservoir or drum below.

Trommel. A revolving sieve for *sizing* ores.
Trouble, NEWC. A dislocation of the strata.
Trow. A wooden channel for air or water.
Trumpeting, S. STAFF. A small channel cut behind the brick-work of a shaft lined with masonry.
Trunk, CORN. A long narrow box or square tube, usually of wood.
Trunking, CORN. Separating slimes by means of a *trunk.*
Tubbing. A shaft-lining of casks or cylindrical caissons, of iron or wood. See *Plank-tubbing.*
Tubing. Lining a deep bore-hole by driving down iron tubes.
Tubs, NEWC. Boxes for lowering coals. See *Trolly.*
Tuff or *Tufa.* A soft sandstone or calcareous deposit.
Tug, DERB. The iron hook of a hoisting bucket, to which the *tacklers* are attached.
Tunnel. 1. A nearly horizontal underground passage, open at both ends to *day.* 2. PAC. See *Adit.*
Tunnel-head. The top of a *shaft-furnace.*
Turbary. A peat-bog.
Turn. A pit sunk in a *drift.*
Turn-bat. A wooden stick used in turning the tongs which hold a *bloom* under the hammer.
Turning-house. The first working on a vein where it has been intersected by a *cross-cut.*
Tut-work. See *Dead-work.* In general, work paid for by the amount of excavation, not (as in *tribute*) of product.
Tuyere, Tweer, Twyer or *Twere.* A pipe inserted in the wall of a furnace, through which the blast is forced into the furnace. Usually the tuyere enters through an embrasure in the masonry (*tuyere-arch*). A *nozzle* or interior pipe is frequently inserted at the inner end of the *tuyere.* By changing the *nozzle,* the size of the opening for the blast may be thus regulated without changing the *tuyere.* The latter is either an annular hollow casting of iron (*box-tuyere*) or bronze (*bronze tuyere*), or a coil of iron pipe. In either case, water is continually circulated through it, to protect it and the nozzle from the action of the melting materials in the furnace. *Spray-tuyeres* are open *box-tuyeres,* in which a spray of water, instead of a current, is employed. This is vaporized by the heat, and passes away as steam.
Tuyere-plate. See *Bloomary.*
Tying, CORN. See *Strake.*
Tymp. A hollow iron casting, cooled interiorly by a current of

water, and placed to protect the *tymp-arch*, or arch over the *dam*, in a blast furnace having a *fore-hearth.* (See *Open front.*)

Under-hand. See *Stope.*

Underlayer, CORN. A vertical shaft sunk to cut a lode.

Underlie or *Underlay*, CORN. The departure of a vein or stratum from the vertical, usually measured in horizontal feet per fathom of inclined depth. Thus a *dip* of 60° is an *underlay* of three feet per fathom. The *underlay* expressed in feet per fathom is six times the natural cosine of the angle of the dip. See *Dip.*

Under-poled copper. Copper not *poled* enough to remove all suboxide.

Universal train. A *roll train* having adjustable horizontal and vertical rolls, so as to produce sections of various sizes.

Unwater. To drain or pump water from a mine.

Upcast. 1. A lifting of a coal seam by a dike. 2. The opening through which the ventilating current passes out of a mine. See *Downcast.*

Upraise. See *Rise.*

Ure's process. The treatment of quicksilver ores by heating in iron retorts with admixture of lime.

Vall' Alta furnace. See *Hühner furnace.*

Vamping. The *débris* of a stope, which forms a hard mass under the feet of the miner.

Vanning, CORN. A method of washing ore on a shovel, analogous to *panning.* Concentrating machines are sometimes called *vanners.* See *Percussion-table.*

Vein. See *Lode.* The term *vein* is also sometimes applied to small threads, or subordinate features of a larger deposit.

Vena, SP. A small vein.

Vend, NEWC. The total sales of coal from a colliery.

Verifier. A tool used in deep boring for detaching and bringing to the surface portions of the wall of the bore-hole at any desired depth.

Vermilion. Mercury sulphide.

Vestry, NEWC. Refuse.

Veta, SP. A vein. As compared with *vena*, *veta* is the main vein.

Viewer. A colliery manager.

Vigorite. See *Explosives.*

92   A GLOSSARY OF MINING AND METALLURGICAL TERMS.

Vug, vugg, or *vugh.* A cavity in the rock, usually lined with a crystalline incrustation. See *Geode.*

Wad-hook. A tool with two spiral steel blades for removing fragments from the bottom of deep bore-holes.

Wagon. A four-wheeled vehicle used in coal mines, usually containing 75 to 100 cubic feet.

Wagon-breast. A *breast* into which wagons can be taken.

Wale, NEWC. To clean coal by picking out the refuse by hand. The boys who do this are called *Walers.*

Wall. 1. The side of a level or drift. 2. The *country-rock* bounding a vein laterally.

Wall-plates, CORN. The two side-pieces of a timber frame in a shaft, parallel to the strike of the lode when the shaft is sunk on the lode. The other two pieces are the *end-pieces.*

Washer. See *Ore-washer.*

Water-jacket. See *Jacket.*

Waste, NEWC. Old workings. The signification seems to include that of both *goaf* and *gob.*

Wastrel. A tract of waste land or any waste material.

Water-barrel or *Water-tank.* A barrel or box, with a self-acting valve at the bottom, used for hoisting water in lieu of a pump.

Water-level. 1. The level at which, by natural or artificial drainage, water is removed from a mine or mineral deposit. 2. A drift at the water-level.

Water-packer. A water-tight packing of leather between the pipe and the walls of a bore-hole.

Way-shaft. See *Blind-shaft.*

Weather-door. A door in a level to regulate the ventilating current.

Weathering. Changing under the effect of continued exposure to atmospheric agencies.

Wedging-curb or *Wedging-crib,* ENG. A *curb* used to make a water-tight packing between the *tubbing* in a shaft and the rock-walls, by means of split *deals,* moss, and wedges, driven in between the *curb* and the rock.

Weld. To join pieces of metal by pressure, at a temperature below that of complete fusion.

Weld-iron. Wrought-iron. See *Iron* and *Steel.*

Weld-steel. See *Steel.*

Well. The crucible of a furnace.

Welsh process. See *English process.*

Wetherill furnace. A furnace with perforated iron bottom, under which a blast is introduced, and upon which zinc-ore (red oxide) is reduced.

Wharl or *Wharr*, NEWC. A sledge for hauling corves in low drifts.

Wheal, CORN. A mine.

Whim or *Whimsey.* A machine for hoisting by means of a vertical drum, revolved by horse or steam power.

Whin or *Whinstone*, NEWC. Basaltic rock; any hard, unstratified rock. In Scotland, greenstone.

Whip. The simplest horse-power hoisting machine, consisting of a fixed pulley and a hoisting rope passing over it, to which the animal is directly attached.

White-ash, PENN. See *Coal.*

White-damp. A poisonous gas sometimes (more rarely than fire-damp or choke-damp, etc.), encountered in coal mines. It has been supposed to contain carbonic oxide, but this is doubtful.

White furnace. See *Howell furnace.*

White-lead. Carbonate of lead.

White tin, CORN. Metallic tin.

Whits or *Witts*, CORN. See *Tin-witts.*

Whitwell stove. A fire-brick hot-blast stove, on the regenerative system.

Whole-working, NEWC. Working where the ground is still whole, i. e., has not been penetrated as yet with breasts. Opposed to *pillar-work*, or the extraction of pillars left to support previous work.

Wild lead. Zinc-blende.

Wicket. A *breast.* See *Breast*, and *Post-and-stall.*

Wimble. A shell-auger used for boring in soft ground.

Win. To extract ore or coal.

Windbore, NEWC. The pipe at the bottom of a set of pumps.

Winch or *Windlass.* A man-power hoisting machine, consisting of a horizontal drum with crank handles.

Winding. Hoisting with a rope and drum.

Winds. See *Winze.*

Winning. 1. A new opening. 2. The portion of a coal field laid out for working.

Winning headways. NEWC. Headways driven to explore and open out the coal seam.

Winze. An interior shaft, usually connecting two levels.

Wood-tin. Tinstone of light wood-color.
Wootz. See *Steel.*
Work. Ore not yet dressed.
Working. See *Labor.* The Spanish and the English term are synonymous in meaning and alike in application. A *working* may be a *shaft, quarry, level, open-cut,* or *stope,* etc.
Working-barrel, CORN. The cylinder in which a pump piston works.
Working home. Working toward the main shaft in extracting ore or coal, as in *longwall retreating.*
Working-out. Working away from the main shaft in extracting ore or coal, as in *longwall advancing.*
Work-lead. See *Base bullion.*

Yellow-ore. CORN. Chalcopyrite. See *Copper ores.*
Yokings. See *Stowces.*

Zawn, CORN. A cavern.
Ziervogel process. The extraction of silver from sulphuret ores or matte by roasting in such a way as to form sulphate of silver, leaching this out with hot water, and precipitating the silver by means of metallic copper.
Zighyr, zigger, or *sicker,* CORN. To percolate, trickle or ooze, as water through a crack. From the GERM., *sickern.*
Zinc-dust. Finely-divided zinc, zinc-oxide, and impurities, incidentally produced in the manufacture of *spelter.* It is sometimes used as an inferior paint (*zinc-gray*).
Zinc-gray. See *Zinc-dust.*
Zinc-ores. Red ore (*zincite,* oxide); *black-jack* (*zinc-blende, sphalerite,* sulphide); *zinc-spar* (*noble calamine,* Smithsonite, carbonate, and *earthy calamine, hydrozincite,* hydrated carbonate); *silicious oxide* (*willemite,* anhydrous, and *calamine,* hydrated silicate).
Zinc-scum. The zinc-silver alloy skimmed from the surface of the bath in the process of desilverization of lead by zinc.
Zinc-white. Oxide of zinc.
Zones. In a shaft-furnace, the different portions (horizontal sections) are called *zones,* and characterized according to the reactions which take place in them, as the *zone of fusion* or *smelting-zone,* the *reduction-zone,* etc.

www.ingramcontent.com/pod-product-compliance
Lightning Source LLC
Chambersburg PA
CBHW032242080426
42735CB00008B/962